THE
MONEY
RESET

THE MONEY RESET

Take control of your money and your life

GEMMA MITCHELL

WILEY

ISBN: 978-1-394-34616-5

A catalogue record for this book is available from the National Library of Australia

Registered Office
John Wiley & Sons Australia, Ltd. Level 4, 600 Bourke Street, Melbourne, VIC 3000, Australia

For details of our global editorial offices, customer services, and more information about Wiley products visit us at www.wiley.com.

Wiley also publishes its books in a variety of electronic formats and by print-on-demand. Some content that appears in standard print versions of this book may not be available in other formats.

Cover design by Wiley
Cover image: © Thiago/Adobe Stock
Your 12-Step Money Reset Plan: © Cetacons/Adobe Stock; © Mr. Stocker/Adobe Stock
Income-generating ideas: © Mr. Stocker/Adobe Stock
Four key bank accounts: © Mr. Stocker/Adobe Stock

Set in 11.5/15.5 pt and Utopia Std, Straive, Chennai, India.

CONTENTS

ABOUT THE AUTHOR

Gemma Mitchell helps people turn financial setbacks into comebacks.

She is passionate about empowering individuals to take control of their financial futures, particularly those navigating major life transitions such as divorce, career shifts or retirement. With over two decades of experience in banking, finance and wealth coaching, Gemma combines practical financial strategies with deep insights into money mindset and behavioural shifts.

Gemma has worked with individuals and businesses across Australia, guiding them through financial planning, money coaching and wealth-building strategies. She is a keynote speaker, workshop facilitator and co-host of the *Australian Finance Podcast*, reaching thousands of listeners each month.

Her career spans financial services, corporate leadership and media, with features in and collaborations with well-known publications and companies both in Australia and globally. She delivers financial literacy workshops and programs designed to help people build confidence, resilience and long-term wealth.

Beyond finance, Gemma is an adventurer at heart — whether hiking remote trails, camping under the stars or indulging in a little luxury getaway. She lives with her two children on the stunning Sunshine Coast in Queensland, Australia, balancing business and life with a mission to change the way people think — and feel — about money.

Find her at gemmamitchell.com.au.

INTRODUCTION

For so many of us, life (our career, relationship, finances), for the most part, flows fairly smoothly. Things are cruising along until suddenly, they're not.

By the time I hit 28, I was married, living in our dream home, working my dream job and about to welcome our first child, then, not long after, our second.

We had the house. The investment property. The boat. The campervan. Annual overseas holidays. Frequent weekends away. More importantly, we felt financially stable. On paper, nearly every box was ticked. We had built our 'dream life.'

On the outside, it was picture perfect. I had done everything 'right', according to the invisible checklist of success inside my head.

But real life rarely follows the fairytale script, and the plot twists in my story started coming thick and fast.

Everything started to unravel when my husband (spoiler alert: ex-husband) had to permanently stop working due to health issues before he turned 40. And then we separated just a few years later — another plot twist that was definitely not part of my grand plan.

That's the issue with invisible checklists that define our 'success' and 'happiness' — the minute something happens that is definitely not on the list, it all unravels.

Through my years of working with clients as a banker, financial adviser and now money coach, I have been privy to the inner workings of homes, finances and families. And I've seen time and time again how 'happily ever afters' take unexpected plot twists that rewrite our next chapter in ways we never imagined.

For even the most primed 'planner' (like myself), life rarely plays out how it does in your head or on your spreadsheet.

Whether it's a relationship breakdown, the loss of a loved one, the end of your career or the start of a new one, these big upheavals are some of the most uncomfortable times of our lives. Every insecurity comes to the surface: Our stability and safety feel shaky, and our self-worth is challenged. These moments shatter the world we knew — emotionally, practically and financially. What once seemed like a clear and concise script, complete with tangible steps and celebrated milestones, feels as though that story was someone else's entirely.

Big events force a financial rethink — a crash course in managing money — while simultaneously demanding a mental money reset and plan.

I've helped countless clients through these challenging times, working with people navigating redundancies, guiding others through medical diagnoses that ended their careers, supporting couples managing finances together, and helping many untangle finances during separations or after the loss of a loved one. I've spent years helping others navigate their plot twists and rebuild their financial lives — so why did I find myself struggling so much when it was my turn?

Simple: I had all the 'theory', but putting it into practice while navigating my own emotions, my ex's emotions and those of my children (not to mention the unsolicited input from people outside the relationship) was completely uncharted territory.

With emotions running high, legal expenses mounting, frequent housing changes and uncertainty creeping into every part of my life, I felt completely out of control, both personally and financially. As someone who had been pretty much mapping out and planning every inch of their life since childhood, this wasn't a feeling I was too familiar with.

Divorce and other plot twists are an opportunity to reset, but they do not come cleanly. They leave behind layers of complexity, responsibilities and emotional baggage. I had spent years building a life with structure and certainty. I had a tight, well-planned future mapped out. And then, suddenly, it was all gone. Every plan, every assumption about what life would look like in the future was wiped out in an instant. I couldn't control the situation, and that feeling — losing control over something so fundamental — was unbearable.

If this is you, just know that your next step doesn't have to feel like an exciting fresh start. And it might be a step you never wanted to take, one forced by loss, upheaval or circumstances far beyond your control.

You might be:

- navigating the heartbreak of losing a partner, trying to figure out how to keep life moving forward
- walking away from an unsafe home and starting over

- drowning in financial stress (juggling debts, bills or a sudden pay cut), feeling like it's too late to break the cycle

- standing at a crossroads, stuck between staying in a life that doesn't fit any more and taking the leap to create something new and true to yourself.

It's okay to be on a roller-coaster of emotions, experiencing frustration and impatience, then fleeting moments of hope and inspiration, followed by fear, guilt and hopelessness.

This book is your reset roadmap. It's a transformation journey: turning a challenging time in your life into the foundation for something extraordinary. This journey goes far beyond crunching numbers or balancing budgets. It's about rebuilding lives that have been turned upside down. What you're about to read was my own money makeover and that of so many of my clients — so I know it works!

Some of you will feel like you're carrying the weight of the world on your shoulders, and that can make seeing a way forward hard. Think of it as just a series of small steps: small, manageable steps. I'm right here with you to help you rebuild, rewrite or completely reinvent your financial story.

My goal isn't to dismiss the hardships you've faced but to help you recognise the strength you already have and the opportunities waiting for you.

Please know that this balance — honouring your past while inspiring your future — is at the heart of every page of this book. You deserve to feel empowered, not overwhelmed, as you take your next steps forward. No matter how you ended up here, the next chapter is yours to write.

This book is structured around 12 actionable steps, each designed to help you move forward with clarity and confidence. We'll start by taking stock of where you are financially and emotionally, identifying what needs to change, and preparing yourself mentally for the journey ahead. From there, we'll refocus on simplifying and strengthening the core building blocks of your financial life: cashflow, budgeting, debt management, insurance and general wealth planning. Finally, we'll move beyond survival mode, shifting from 'just getting by' to 'what's possible?'

It's important to remember that this is your journey. Only you know where you are starting from, what you're capable of right now and how much you can take on.

This isn't a race and there's no finish line you need to sprint towards. Life is unpredictable. Sometimes you'll move quickly, making progress that feels easy and exciting. Other times, you may need to pause, catch your breath and take things one tiny step at a time — and that's okay. This 12-step plan is here to guide you, not to rush you.

Each step is designed to be flexible, adaptable to your life and focused on building sustainable habits that work for you. Whether you complete it in 12 weeks, six months or a year, the goal is to keep moving forward in a way that feels manageable and empowering. Small, consistent actions will get you closer to where you want to be — and those small actions add up to big changes over time.

Ready?

How to use this book

Progress isn't about perfection; it's about persistence. This book is designed to help you focus on what's next, not everything at once. It's not about going from zero to 100 overnight. It's about putting one foot in front of the other, step by step, decision by decision.

That's exactly where *The Money Reset* comes in.

But how you use it is up to you.

Whether you want a deep dive, a quick reset or just a place to start, there's a way forward that works for your time, energy and situation.

If you just need a starting point: Dip in and out as needed

- Skim through the book to get a sense of the framework.

- Focus on Chapters 1 and 2 to help you take stock of where you are and what needs to change.

- Come back to the other chapters when you're ready: this book is here as a long-term resource, not a one-time checklist.

If you need a fast-track reset: Pick the chapters that matter most

- Scan the table of contents and choose the areas that resonate with you right now.

- Focus on those key chapters first: maybe it's budgeting, income or rebuilding after a big change.

- Use the exercises that feel relevant, and don't worry about completing everything in order.

If you're all in: Follow the full 12-step plan

Read through each chapter, taking time to reflect and complete the exercises. Expect some steps to take longer than others. This isn't about rushing; it's about real change.

There's no 'right' way to do this, only what works for you.

No matter how long it takes, the goal is to keep moving forward. Every small step adds up.

Let's get started with an overview of the 12 steps on the next page.

Your 12-Step Money Reset Plan

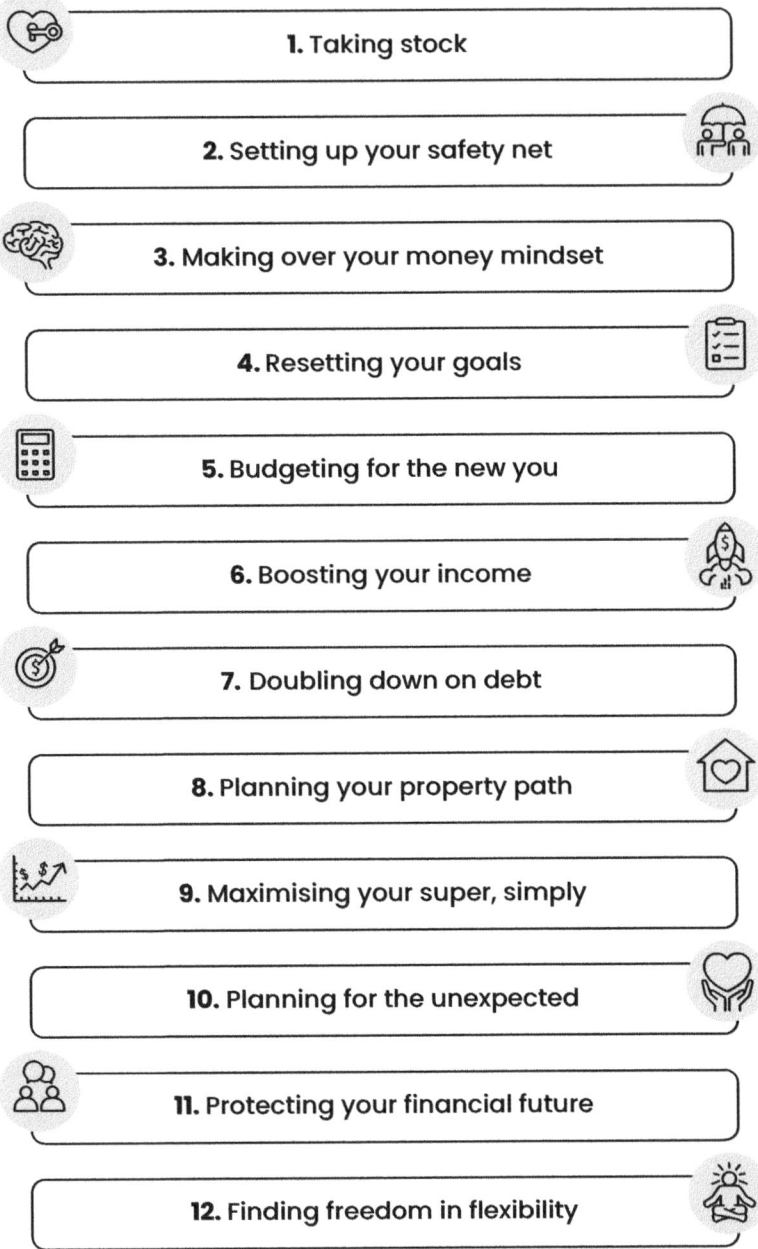

1. Taking stock

2. Setting up your safety net

3. Making over your money mindset

4. Resetting your goals

5. Budgeting for the new you

6. Boosting your income

7. Doubling down on debt

8. Planning your property path

9. Maximising your super, simply

10. Planning for the unexpected

11. Protecting your financial future

12. Finding freedom in flexibility

The reset

Life doesn't always go to plan. We set goals, build stability and map out our future, only to be hit with a plot twist — whether it's a divorce, job loss, financial mess or one of those moments that make you stop and rethink everything. These moments can feel like everything's falling apart, but they also hold a strange kind of power. They force us to pause, reassess and, if we let them, reset in a way that actually works for who we are now and who we are becoming.

Before diving into financial decisions, it's important to take a step back. Without that pause, choices can feel rushed, messy or purely reactive. I know firsthand how easy it is to power through, convincing yourself that action — any action — is better than stopping. But moving too fast can lead to decisions that backfire, like taking on unnecessary debt, making financial commitments you're not ready for or jumping into something you'll later regret.

On the flip side, freezing in place might feel like the safest bet. If you don't move, you can't mess up, right? But staying stuck in that in-between space doesn't help either. It keeps you in limbo, waiting for things to magically fix themselves, which, spoiler alert, they won't.

The sweet spot is in the middle: pausing with purpose. Take a moment to breathe, take stock and make sure that when you do move forward, you're not just reacting, but actually choosing your next steps.

This reset is about getting clear on where you're currently at — financially and emotionally — and moving forward with intention. It's about making sure that when you do act, it's the right action for you.

Resilience is built right here, in the space where you choose to reset instead of just react.

So let's go!

Chapter 1
Taking stock

When life throws challenges your way, it's natural to feel stuck, frustrated or even a little lost — especially if you're not where you thought you would be in your life. Maybe you're navigating the fallout of a big life change or you're starting to realise that the things that worked for you before just don't any more. Whatever the case, it's okay to stop and acknowledge those feelings. In fact, it's necessary.

Before you can move forward, it's so important to take a moment and honestly acknowledge where you are right now. And no, this isn't about beating yourself up or getting stuck in regret — it's about looking at your current situation with clarity and compassion. Think of it as hitting pause to get your bearings before figuring out your next steps. Otherwise, it's like trying to follow a map without knowing your starting point.

This kind of reflection isn't always easy. It can bring up truths you'd rather avoid or force you to let go of old ideas and expectations that no longer fit your reality. And while that can feel confronting, it's also where the magic happens. It's empowering to look at where you are — not with judgement but with the intention to understand and grow. As Maya Angelou is purported to have said, 'Do the best you can until you know better. Then when you know better, do better.'

Our life and financial goals are often shaped by a mix of conscious intentions and unconscious beliefs we've picked up over time. From a young age, we absorb ideas about money, success and security from our families, culture and community. These influences (whether helpful or limiting) form the narrative that guides our decisions, often without us even realising it.

How grief appears in everyday life

One theme that comes up again and again — in my own life and with the clients I work with — is grief. Grief doesn't just come from losing someone you love. It can show up when you let go of an old dream, a former identity or a version of your life you thought you'd have.

Grief doesn't always show up the way we expect. It can be sneaky. Sometimes, it's loud and all-consuming, impossible to ignore. Other times, it lingers quietly in the background, like a shadow influencing your thoughts, choices and behaviours in ways you don't even realise.

Psychiatrist Elisabeth Kübler-Ross introduced the well-known five stages of grief: denial, anger, bargaining, depression and acceptance. Over time, this model has been expanded to include emotions like shock, guilt, loneliness and even reconstruction. But one of the biggest misconceptions about these stages is that they happen in a neat, linear order, that you move through them one by one and then come out the other side. In reality, grief doesn't work like that. Kübler-Ross herself later clarified that these emotions come in waves, overlapping, repeating and sometimes hitting you when you least expect it.

One thing I've learned is that grief, transformation and financial growth are all interconnected. Doing the work in one area often creates a ripple effect in the others.

Understanding these stages won't take away the discomfort, but it can help you make sense of what you're feeling and remind you that you're not alone. What you're experiencing is completely valid, and no matter how overwhelming it feels, it's part of the process of finding your way forward.

Grief is messy, transformation is messy, and these emotions don't follow a straight path. It would be a lot easier if they did! But knowing that it's okay to move back and forth, to feel like you're making progress one day and stuck the next, can take some of the pressure off. This isn't about rushing through emotions; it's about allowing yourself to move through them in the way that feels right for you.

In my own money journey, emotions such as sadness, guilt, anger and doubt still pop up uninvited. Sometimes they make me feel like I'm treading water — or even drowning. But I'm learning not to resist them. When those feelings surface, I pause, acknowledge them and come back to my 'why'. (That's something we'll dive into more in Chapter 4.)

Just know this: Acknowledging where you are isn't a weakness. It's the first step towards clarity and your financial foundation for meaningful progress.

Reframe and reimagine

Let's start with a *big* question: *How do you honestly feel right now?*

Maybe you're overwhelmed by how far away your financial goals feel. Maybe you're frustrated by the choices that led you here, or unsure how to even take the first step forward. For many, this isn't the kind of fresh start that feels exhilarating — it's the one you never wanted, forced by loss, upheaval or circumstances beyond your control.

And that's okay. Feeling that mix of emotions (overwhelm, frustration, grief) is part of the process. It's important to give yourself permission to feel all of it without guilt or judgement. But here's the thing: While your situation might not look like what you envisioned, it's also an opportunity. This is your chance to reimagine what's possible.

Reframing doesn't mean ignoring how hard things are. It's not about pretending everything's fine or sugar-coating your struggles. It's about acknowledging where you are while intentionally shifting your perspective towards what's possible.

The way you view your circumstances has a powerful impact on how you respond to them. If you see your challenges as impossible, it's easy to stay stuck, paralysed by fear or frustration. But if you choose to see them as an opportunity to grow, learn or rebuild, suddenly the path forward becomes clearer — even if it's still uncertain.

Reframing lets you shift your mindset and take back control. It's about moving from:

- 'This is so unfair' to 'This is my chance to rebuild in a way that truly works for me'
- 'I didn't choose this' to 'I *can* choose what happens next'
- 'I'll never catch up' to 'I can make progress, one small step at a time.'

Throughout this book, I'll share my own stories of reframing, sometimes serious, where the need to reframe was a hard and unavoidable necessity, and other times a bit more lighthearted and tongue-in-cheek. Both have their place, and both have helped me rewrite the way I approach life's unexpected plot twists.

Your mindset is one of the most powerful tools you have. Shifting your perspective doesn't erase the challenges you're facing. It just helps you approach them with intention and strength.

Here are four simple steps to do that:

First, acknowledge the hard truths. It's okay to admit that this isn't where you thought you'd be or that you didn't choose to be here. Recognising that reality isn't a sign of failure; it's a vital part of your story. It's about giving yourself permission to say, 'This is where I am, and that's okay.'

Next, focus on what's within your control. You might not have chosen this path or been able to control what brought you here, but you *can* control how you move forward. Shift your energy to the things you can influence: your habits, your mindset, your daily actions. Regaining a sense of agency, no matter how small, is incredibly empowering.

Start visualising what's possible. Instead of letting your thoughts spiral around what you've lost, ask yourself, *What could I build from here?* What would your life look like if you started taking even the smallest steps towards something better today?

Finally, find strength in your story. This chapter of your life may not have been part of the plan, but it's still a chapter worth writing. This is your chance to create a story of resilience, transformation and growth. You're not just surviving; you're rebuilding with intention.

Reframing isn't about ignoring the pain or pretending everything is easy. It's about giving yourself permission to see this moment as an opening, a space where something new can grow. It's about trusting that your story isn't over—it's evolving, and you're in the driver's seat.

Take it one step at a time, and let this chapter be one that inspires not just recovery, but a reinvention of who you are and what's possible for your life.

Reset now: Reframe your position

Pause and check in with yourself.

First, acknowledge the hard truths about your current situation. Write down three words that describe how you're feeling right now—no filtering, just the truth. These could be that you feel hopeful, overwhelmed, stressed, inspired or determined.

1. _____

2. _____

3. _____

Next, focus on what's within your control. What can you control and what might you need to let go of?

_____

_____

_____

Then, start visualising what's possible. How do you want to feel by the end of this book? By the end of one month or 12 months from now?

_____

_____

_____

Change is a choice

The powerful thing about transformation is that your life can shift faster than you think. In just one year, your career, relationships, routines and finances could look completely different. The key is recognising your worth, believing you deserve better and taking small, consistent steps to move forward. It's not about waiting for the 'right time'. It's about trusting that even the smallest intentional actions can create big, meaningful change.

So why do so many people hesitate to take that first step? Why does change, especially when it comes to financial security, feel so overwhelming? The reasons are often deeply personal, but also incredibly common.

For some, the challenge is simply not knowing where to begin. When life feels chaotic or the road ahead is unclear, it's easier to push things to a distant 'someday' that never arrives. Others are carrying so much already (work, family, responsibilities) that finances get pushed further down the to-do list.

Then there's the belief that things will work themselves out. While hope is a powerful emotion, it's not a plan. Life is unpredictable, and waiting for stability to arrive on its own can leave you vulnerable to unexpected turns.

For many, money—especially investing or long-term planning—can feel intimidating. Keeping cash safe in a bank account feels easier than figuring out how to grow it. Others rely on a partner for financial stability, assuming that security will always be there. While relationships can provide support, true security comes from knowing you can stand on your own if you need to.

In the pages ahead, we'll explore how your mindset, habits and financial patterns shape your future. But, for now, just know that moving forward doesn't mean you have to fix everything overnight. It starts with one small decision today, then another tomorrow. Those choices will build momentum, and before you know it, you'll be in a completely different place.

Transformation doesn't need perfect conditions. You can hit the reset button at any time. You don't need to wait for 1 January, a Monday or even a shiny new notebook. You can start transforming your life on a completely ordinary Wednesday night. The timing doesn't matter — what matters is that you start.

Every single day, you're presented with a choice: stay where you are (stuck in the familiar) or take a step (no matter how small) towards growth and change.

I love the saying 'Choose your hard'. It's such a simple yet powerful reminder that no path is without its challenges, but we always have the power to decide which challenges are worth the discomfort.

- Being financially disciplined is hard; change is hard.
- Starting a business is hard; working for someone else is hard.
- Keeping fit is hard; being unfit is hard.
- Leaving a toxic relationship is hard; staying in one is hard.
- Learning new skills is hard; staying stagnant is hard.

Choose your hard.

The truth is, change *is* messy. It's uncomfortable and often filled with moments where you second-guess yourself. The old ways, even when they're not serving you any more, can feel oddly safe, like that worn-out jumper you keep in the back of the wardrobe. Letting go of those old habits, beliefs and patterns can feel like giving up a piece of yourself. But here's the thing: Holding onto what's not helping you won't make moving forward any easier.

Ask yourself: If nothing changes, what does life look like a day, a week or even a year from now? Am I okay with that?

If the answer is no, then it's time to make a choice: not a perfect choice, not a monumental leap, just a single step. The timing doesn't have to be perfect, and you don't have to have it all figured out. Transformation isn't about having all the answers upfront; it's about deciding today that you're ready to start.

And the truth is, you've already started. Reading this, reflecting on it, letting yourself think about what could be different — that's a step. So give yourself credit for that. Every small step counts, and those small steps? They're what add up to the big shifts over time.

Reset now: Rewrite your narrative

Grab a pen and write down three areas of your life that feel hard and that you want to change. Some of these might be 'I don't want to worry about not being able to pay rent on time' or 'I want to be able to say yes to more fun in my life'.

1. _____

2. _____

3. _____

What's your net worth?

Once you've acknowledged where you're at emotionally, and looked at some narratives you might like to rewrite, it's time to acknowledge where you are at financially: your current net worth. Calculating your net worth is a key first step to resetting your finances and creating a clear plan to take you where you want to go.

Think of it like stepping on a financial scale or finding your spot on the map before starting a journey. It's your starting line in a race — and I mean a marathon, not a sprint! Your net worth tells you where you are right now, but it's not a prediction of where you're headed or, importantly, a reflection of who you are.

Your net worth is a snapshot, not a selfie. It gives you a clear picture of your financial position at a specific moment in time and provides a baseline for tracking your progress. But here's the critical bit: It doesn't define your value as a person.

Repeat after me: 'My net worth is not my self-worth.'

I remember calculating my net worth after my financial settlement (the final step of my separation) was finalised — it was a strange, confronting and overwhelming experience... but not in a bad way. It was like standing in the ruins of what once was, and for the first time, really seeing the landscape clearly. There was something unexpectedly inspiring about it. Yes, everything had changed. Yes, it was confronting to see the numbers so starkly. But it was also powerful — because now I knew exactly where I stood.

It was my starting point — clear, tangible and *mine*. Even if my net worth wasn't what it once was, it felt freeing to know exactly where I stood. From that point, I could stop feeling like I was in limbo and finally start moving forward.

So how do you do it? It's a simple equation:

Your assets – your liabilities = your net worth

Let's start with your assets.

Your assets are what you own, and they contribute positively to your net worth. Some examples include:

- *Cash and savings:* Money in your checking, savings and high-interest savings accounts.

- *Investments:* Shares, bonds, exchange traded funds (ETFs) and retirement accounts like superannuation, KiwiSaver or 401(k).

- *Property:* Your home, investment properties or land you own.

- *Vehicles:* Cars, motorcycles, boats, caravans (but keep in mind these depreciate over time, so if you want to leave them out, like I do in my own calculations, then go ahead).

- *Valuables:* Jewellery, art, collectables or other tangible items of significant value that could be sold.

- *Business ownership:* Value in a business that you could sell.

Then we have your liabilities.

Liabilities are what you owe money for, and they reduce your net worth. Common liabilities include:

- *Mortgages:* The outstanding balance on any property loans.

- *Student loans:* Education-related debt.

- *Credit card debt:* Any balances not paid off.

- *Personal loans:* Borrowed money from banks, friends or family.

- *Car loans:* Outstanding amounts on vehicle financing.

- *Other obligations:* Buy-now-pay-later debts, medical bills, tax debts or other financial commitments.

You'll see from these lists that I have included your home as an asset and, for our purposes, it is an asset. If you were to look at your net worth in terms of assets that might *provide you with financial freedom*, the value of your home often doesn't count. Why? Because unless you're planning to sell it, downsize or rent it out, your home *isn't generating income*. It's valuable, yes, and it's hopefully an asset growing in value, but it's not one that's actively working for your financial future.

That being said, if you plan to keep your home and it has a mortgage that needs to be paid off, then the loan needs to be included as a liability.

If you include your home in your net worth, you might see a nice positive number. Exclude it, especially if you're carrying a mortgage (which needs to stay in!), and it's likely you will see a dip into the negative. That's okay! The goal here is clarity.

Reset now: Work out your net worth

Grab a pen and list all of your current assets (cash, investments, property) and liabilities (mortgage, loans, credit cards).

ASSETS		LIABILITIES	
Description	Value	Description	Value
Total:		Total:	
Notes		**NET WORTH**	
		Total assets:	
		Total liabilities:	
		Total net worth:	

You could also do this in a basic spreadsheet — it doesn't have to be complicated. Prefer an online tool? Check out the Moneysmart net worth calculator at moneysmart.gov.au.

Today's date: _____ My net worth is $_____

The big picture

While this may be the first time (or the first time in a long time) that you've calculated your net worth, it's not a one-and-done exercise. Think of tracking your net worth like getting a yearly check-up: It's an opportunity to see how far you've come, make small adjustments and ensure your financial path aligns with your evolving life.

For most people, checking in annually is enough to see meaningful progress without stressing over short-term fluctuations. But if you're working towards a major financial goal (paying off debt, investing aggressively or navigating a life transition), more frequent check-ins (maybe quarterly) might be a powerful motivator.

The key is to find a rhythm that keeps you engaged without letting the numbers define your success or self-worth. Your net worth is simply a reflection of where you are today, not a measure of your potential or your future. Each check-in is an opportunity to celebrate wins, learn from challenges and refine your path forward.

Remember, this is your starting line — your race, your pace! It's a marathon, not a sprint, and you're the only one in it.

Chapter 2

Setting up your safety net

You've probably heard the phrase 'Money can't buy happiness'. In my opinion, this phrase isn't entirely true.

While happiness isn't solely about material things, financial security and resources play a huge role in your overall wellbeing and quality of life. When you can consistently meet your basic needs and pay your bills, the stress starts to lift, creating space for you to focus on the things that truly bring joy.

Financial stability doesn't just ease your worries; it creates freedom. It opens doors to opportunities, and it gives you the power to make decisions that aren't driven purely by monetary constraints.

Having money, or managing the money you do have, also means you can make bold choices — like leaving a toxic workplace or unsafe relationship — without feeling trapped by fear of financial instability.

Ultimately, money gives you the power to align your decisions with your values, lifestyle and priorities. While it may not guarantee happiness, it ensures there are fewer roadblocks in the way for you to create your own happiness.

Security isn't just about having money in the bank or ticking off boxes on a financial to-do list. It's about creating a sense of calm and control in your life. It's knowing that, no matter what happens, you have a foundation strong enough to weather the storm.

Money on its own can't solve every problem, but let's not underestimate the peace of mind that comes with financial stability. It's hard to thrive when you're stuck in survival mode, constantly consumed by the what-ifs.

You need to shift from reactive to proactive. Build a new financial baseline that lets you breathe easier and move through life with confidence and safety.

Your safety is a non-negotiable

Let's start with this: *You deserve to feel safe and secure.* Not someday, not when you hit a milestone, but right now. And that sense of security doesn't have to come from extravagant wealth or perfectly managing every dollar. It's about creating some non-negotiables — key measures that allow you to rest easy and live your life without the constant weight of uncertainty.

When it comes to feeling safe and secure, everyone should have their own list of non-negotiables — those essential things that create a sense of stability, no matter what's happening in the world around you. These are the financial (and often emotional) safety measures that give you confidence and peace of mind. They're personal, practical and deeply connected to what matters most to *you.*

If you're not quite there yet, and the idea of having your non-negotiables covered feels like a distant goal, that's okay. This isn't about where you are today; it's about identifying what's important to you so that you have a clear focus moving forward.

For me, my non-negotiables have evolved over time, shaped by life's ups and downs. I didn't always have them covered, and there were times when meeting even one felt out of reach. But over the years, I've come to realise that these are the things I need to feel safe and secure:

- safe housing for me and my kids
- food on the table — always
- access to money in case of an emergency
- my kids' schooling paid for, so their education is never at risk.

By looking at my non-negotiables, I can clearly see that my income is a major player in ensuring I can meet all of these, so protecting my income with insurance (we'll dive into this in Chapter 10) is a must for me.

Those are mine, but your non-negotiables might look completely different. You might have two or you might have ten. Maybe for you, it's knowing your mortgage or rent is covered each month. Perhaps it's keeping up the maintenance of a campervan you live in full time as you travel Australia. Maybe it's keeping a specific amount in your savings account, ensuring you always have health or pet insurance, or staying out of debt.

The point isn't to adopt someone else's list. It's to figure out what *you* need to feel secure. Your non-negotiables should reflect your values, your lifestyle and the things that allow you to feel calm, focused and in control.

Here are a few more examples of what non-negotiables might look like:

- always paying your bills on time
- having at least three months' worth of expenses for essentials saved
- maintaining a strong credit score for future opportunities
- always having funds for a particular membership
- investing in regular health check-ups or private health insurance
- staying debt-free or avoiding high-interest debt like credit cards
- setting aside money for personal growth, such as education or professional development.

Feeling safe and secure isn't just something you want — it's something you deserve.

Reset now: List your non-negotiables

Take a moment to list your non-negotiables according to where you're at right now in your life.

1. _____

2. _____

3. _____

4. _____

5. _____

A solid foundation

Defining your non-negotiables is a personal process, and it's okay if they change over time. What feels essential during one chapter of your life may shift as your circumstances and goals evolve. The key is to regularly check in with yourself and adjust as needed.

Your non-negotiables guide your decisions and help you prioritise where your money goes. Once you've identified your non-negotiables, they become the foundation for your financial plan. These non-negotiables may even highlight areas that turn into actionable goals, like 'build an emergency fund' or 'pay off debt', and that's great. It will make the process of setting goals so much easier if you can refer back to these non-negotiables when we get to goal setting.

More importantly, your non-negotiables serve as an anchor during challenging times, giving you clarity and focus when uncertainty creeps in.

Your emergency fund

Before we move on, we need to cover one of the most important non-negotiables for almost everyone: your emergency fund.

It's the ultimate safety net and one of the most powerful tools you can build to protect your financial security, which is why it's important to focus fully on it here.

Emergencies happen. One minute you're cruising through a busy week, and the next, your water heater dies. Or worse—it's the middle of a Queensland summer, and your air conditioner gives out. While these are minor inconveniences, they're frustrating, often expensive and always ill-timed. Then there are the bigger, more serious moments: leaving an unsafe home, walking away from a toxic job or dealing with an injury that stops you from working.

Unexpected expenses don't just strain your wallet; they come with emotional and logistical challenges too. That's where having a financial safety net makes all the difference.

When you know you've got funds set aside, you can focus on *solving* the problem, not just stressing about how to pay for it. Whether it's a sudden medical bill or an urgent home repair, an emergency fund keeps you calm and in control.

It's not just a backup plan; it's your protection against setbacks. You've worked hard to build your financial future, and an emergency fund ensures one unexpected expense won't undo your progress. Think of it as your safety harness: there when you need it, allowing you to navigate life's challenges with confidence. Remember, you deserve to feel safe and secure!

An emergency fund isn't just about having money stashed away; it's about knowing you've got resources to handle life's surprises without throwing your entire financial plan off track.

How much to calculate

Most finance professionals will recommend you save three to six months' worth of your expenses as an emergency stash. Now, it's common for people to panic when they hear 'three to six months' because it can feel like a huge and very unattainable target, especially if your current emergency account is sitting at zero.

Importantly, your emergency fund doesn't have to replace your full income — it just needs to cover your *baseline living expenses.*

While the general recommendation is three to six months' worth of essential costs, this can vary depending on your circumstances. If your job is stable, you have unused entitlements such as sick leave or annual leave, and no dependents, three months' worth might feel sufficient. If you're self-employed, supporting a family or have unpredictable income, aiming for six months (or more) may feel more reasonable.

For me, being single, renting and with significantly reduced assets after my divorce, the amount I needed in my emergency fund was much larger than what I previously felt comfortable with to pass my sleep-at-night test (more on that on page 24).

Only you can work out what feels right.

In Chapter 5, we'll dive into exactly how to determine your expenses, which will help you work out the right amount for your emergency fund. But, for now, start with a smaller, more achievable goal. Aim for $1000 as your first milestone — it's enough to cover many common emergencies and gives you a solid win to build momentum.

Think of it as a stepping stone. For example:

- first $1000: covers basic unexpected expenses such as car repairs or a medical bill
- $1500: a little extra breathing room for bigger setbacks
- $2500: starting to feel a real financial cushion
- building one month of expenses: a stronger buffer against bigger disruptions.

It won't happen overnight, and that's okay. The key is consistency. What's a realistic first goal for you? Would setting aside $50 a week get you there in your target number of months? Could you stretch to $100 a week and hit your goal sooner?

Pick a number that feels doable and commit to getting started.

The key is to start small and focus on consistent contributions: Even $50 or $100 a month adds up over time.

Reset now: What will be your first goal?

1. What is in your current emergency fund (if anything)?

   _____

   _____

2. How much would make a good first savings milestone to build up your emergency fund?

   _____

   _____

Use it but replenish it

Your emergency fund needs to be accessible — but not too accessible. Keep it separate from your everyday spending so you're not tempted to dip in for non-essentials. An account that's not linked to a bank card or credit card works well — it's there when you need it but out of easy reach.

You know what also helps? Defining your own version of an emergency.

To me, an emergency is a car breakdown, urgent home repairs, medical bills or unexpected vet expenses — things that *have* to be covered and can't wait.

Emergencies are not a little wardrobe update, a weekend away with friends or replacing your perfectly good phone just because a newer model has been released.

If you find yourself in a real emergency, one that checks off your definition of emergency, don't hesitate to use your fund — that's exactly what this money is for. It's there to help you navigate tough times without relying on debt or derailing your financial goals.

Remember the golden rule of an emergency fund: *Use it when you need it.*

Your emergency fund is one of the most powerful tools you can have for financial security. It's not just about the money. It's about giving yourself the confidence to face whatever comes next, knowing you're prepared and protected.

If you dip into it (which is exactly what it's there for), just remember to top it back up. This money is your safety net, not a one-way credit line. Think of it like refuelling your car after a long drive — you want to be ready to go again when life takes an unexpected turn.

Reset now: What's an emergency for you?

Write it down now so when the moment comes, you'll know exactly when to use your fund (and when to leave it alone).

_____

_____

_____

Make replenishing your emergency fund a priority. Treat it like paying off a loan to yourself, so it's there and ready for next time.

Your sleep-at-night test

If you listen to any of my podcasts, take part in my courses or bump into me at social gatherings (yes, I'm *that* person at a party), you will hear me constantly bang on about the concept of your 'sleep-at-night test'. Why? Because it's that important!

Every decision you make from this point on needs to make sure you can sleep well at night.

Life is too short to spend your nights staring at the ceiling, worrying if you've made the right move. Financial decisions (big or small) should give you a sense of peace, not panic. But, and this is important, let's not confuse peace of mind with avoiding discomfort. Growth is uncomfortable. Change is uncomfortable. They're supposed to be.

If you're on a journey to transform your life — whether that's your finances, career or relationships — there will be moments that feel hard. That's just part of the process. Growth requires us to step into the unknown, and the unknown can feel messy and unsettling. So the sleep-at-night test isn't about using discomfort as an excuse to stay in your comfort zone.

The real key here is balance. There's a difference between feeling stretched because you're growing and feeling stressed because you're going against your instincts.

The sleep-at-night test helps you distinguish between the discomfort of change (which is temporary and often necessary) and the deep, gnawing stress that comes from knowing a decision doesn't align with your values or goals.

Every decision you make will generally have a trade-off, and when it comes to managing your finances, the trade-off shouldn't be lack of sleep. Your finances shouldn't keep you up at night, and if they do, it's a clear sign something needs to change.

For example, let's say you've decided to start saving more aggressively for an emergency fund. That might mean cutting back on things you enjoy temporarily — eating out less or skipping that weekend getaway — and, yes, that's uncomfortable. But if the decision to save aligns with your goals and passes your sleep-at-night test, it's discomfort with a purpose.

On the other hand, if you're saving in a way that feels extreme, unsustainable or misaligned with your needs, and it's keeping you awake at night, that's a sign you need to reassess.

The sleep-at-night test is about finding that middle ground. It's not about avoiding tough decisions, but it's also not about pushing yourself so hard that your mental and emotional wellbeing suffers.

The sleep-at-night test is about making choices that challenge you while still allowing you to feel secure and confident about the path you're taking.

Your critical questions

The beauty of having a sleep-at-night test is that it's personal. After all, it's your sleep you are protecting! You know yourself better than anyone else. You know what matters to you, what makes you feel secure and what gives you that deep-down feeling of *this is right for me.*

To get started, here's a list of ten questions. Your job is to pick the three that resonate most with you. These will become your go-to filters whenever you're faced with a tough decision.

- Will this decision create more peace or stress in my life?
- Do I have all the information I need to make this decision?
- Am I staying true to my values and long-term goals?
- Am I basing my decision on emotions or facts?
- If I fast forward a month (or a year), will I feel good about this choice?
- Would I feel comfortable recommending this decision to a close friend or loved one?
- Does this decision support my future self?
- Will this choice make me feel secure, or will it leave me feeling uncertain?
- Does this align with the financial foundation I'm building?
- Am I rushing into this decision, or have I given myself time to think it through?

Maybe you're someone who values peace and clarity, so you'll focus on whether a decision creates more peace or stress. Or maybe your big driver is staying aligned with your values and goals, so you'll choose questions that help you check in with those. There's no right or wrong answer; it's about what feels *right* for you.

It's about being honest with yourself, trusting your instincts and making decisions that stretch you in the right way.

Reset now: Create your sleep-at-night test

What are your three questions that make up your sleep-at-night test?

Circle the ones in the list that you feel most aligned with. Write your three questions somewhere you will see them: create notes in your phone, put them on a screensaver on your laptop, or a leave sticky note on your car visor.

1. _____

2. _____

3. _____

The next time you're faced with a choice, pause and ask yourself these three questions.

If it passes your sleep-at-night test, even if it feels uncomfortable, you'll know you're on the right track. And if it doesn't? That's your sign to step back, reassess and explore alternatives that feel better for you.

Build your village

The next crucial part of feeling safe and secure is building your support system, because, as they say, it takes a village.

Rebuilding your financial life (or any part of your life) isn't something you have to do alone. Sure, you probably could do it solo. But should you? Could you do it better, faster or with more confidence by having the right support? Absolutely.

Let's be honest: Going it alone *feels* easier at first. You don't have to explain yourself, show your vulnerabilities or confront any of the guilt or shame that often comes with money. Asking for help can feel like admitting you don't have it all figured out. But here's the truth: Having support doesn't mean you're weak. It means you're smart enough to know that growth is a team effort.

Whether it's emotional support, accountability or professional guidance, surrounding yourself with the right people can make all the difference. The right support system can help you stay on track, make better decisions and remind you that you're not alone in this.

Having a village isn't just a nice-to-have — it's a game changer. Here's what the right support system can offer:

- *Perspective:* Sometimes we're so close to a problem that we can't see the full picture. Someone else, whether that's a friend, mentor or professional, can offer fresh insights or help you see options you might not have considered.

- *Accountability:* Let's face it; it's easier to stick to your goals when you've shared them with someone else. Whether it's a financial coach, a partner or even a friend, having someone check in on your progress can keep you motivated and focused.

- *Encouragement:* On the tough days, when doubt creeps in or things feel overwhelming, the right people can remind you why you started and cheer you on.

- *Guidance:* Professionals, like financial advisers or money coaches, can provide the expertise and structure you need to move forward with confidence. They help you avoid costly mistakes and ensure you're on the best path for your unique situation.

Your village doesn't need to be big. It just needs to be strong. The people you surround yourself with should lift you up, support your goals and provide value in their own unique way. Here's what a well-rounded village might look like:

- *Cheerleaders:* These are the friends or family members who believe in you, no matter what. They might not have financial expertise, but they're your biggest fans and will remind you how far you've come.

- *Accountability partners:* These are the people who keep you on track, whether it's a friend you check in with weekly, a money coach who helps you stay focused or a partner who shares your financial goals.

- *Experts:* Think of financial advisers, accountants or even legal professionals. These are the people who bring expertise and help you make informed decisions. They're not emotionally tied to your situation, which makes their advice objective and valuable. The moneysmart.gov.au website is a great place to start for help finding the right experts.

- *Mentors:* This could be someone you admire who's been through a similar journey. They've walked the path before you, and their experience can offer insights, guidance and inspiration.

- *Like-minded community:* Being part of a group of people with similar goals can be incredibly motivating. This could be a support group, a social media community or even a book club focused on personal growth.

Here's the part that's often the hardest: letting people in. Asking for help requires vulnerability, and that can feel uncomfortable. But vulnerability isn't a weakness; it's a strength. It shows that you're willing to do what it takes to grow and succeed, even if that means admitting you don't have all the answers.

Having a village doesn't mean you're handing over control. You're still the driver of this journey. But having a strong support system means you've got passengers who can help navigate with you, cheer you on and remind you how far you've come.

It's also important to remember that your village might evolve over time. The people with you at the beginning of your journey might not be there at the end, and that's not a bad thing. Outgrowing certain relationships or connections doesn't mean you're ungrateful for their support. It simply means you're moving into a new phase. Growth often comes with shedding old layers, and that includes relationships that no longer align with your path.

As you grow, your needs and priorities will change, and the people you surround yourself with should reflect that growth.

Reset now: Nominate your village

Take a moment to think about your village. Who's already there, supporting you? Who might you need to add?

Who is your cheerleader?

_____

_____

Who is your accountability partner?

_____

_____

What experts do you currently have helping?

_____

_____

What experts might you need to add?

_____

_____

Who is someone you look up to about money?

_____

_____

Who are like-minded people or supports?

_____

_____

Who is missing?

_____

_____

I go into more detail about some of the professionals you may want to add to your village on page 233.

Be safe online

Support is invaluable, but you should always be mindful of your boundaries and privacy, especially when it comes to finances online.

If you're sharing in online communities or seeking advice in public forums, keep your personal details high level and protect your privacy. Vulnerability doesn't mean you have to share *everything*. Be cautious, stay safe and remember that not every space is the right one for your journey.

Here are some examples of what you *could* share in online groups or public forums to help celebrate wins or seek accountability:

- *Your goals.* For example, 'I'm working on saving my emergency fund by the end of the year.'

- *Small wins.* Such as, 'I saved $200 this month by cutting back on eating out', or 'I finally started a budget!'
- *General challenges.* For example, 'I'm struggling to stick to my spending plan', or 'Does anyone have tips for saving on groceries?'
- *Motivational milestones.* For example, 'I paid off one of my credit cards today!' or 'I reached 50 per cent of my savings goal!'

But there is a lot you *shouldn't* share in public or with people you're unsure about. Your personal information can be used to manipulate you, take advantage of you and scam you, so I want you to get support, but be safe with what you share. Here are just a few examples.

- *Exact financial details.* For example, 'My investment is now at $X with [institution]'.
- *Personal identifiers.* Your full name, address, bank details or anything sensitive.
- *Detailed financial struggles.* 'I'm three months behind on rent' should be kept private.
- *Highly personal financial plans.* Talk to a professional about things like withdrawing from retirement funds, not a public forum.

If you are ever unsure, don't share it! Your supporters don't need details to be able to keep you on track or accountable.

Building financial security isn't just about numbers in a bank account — it's about giving yourself the foundation to live with confidence, clarity and control.

When you have your non-negotiables covered, an emergency fund in place and a support system around you, you're no longer reacting to life's financial challenges — you're proactively shaping your future.

Chapter 3

Making over your money mindset

Our relationship with money begins at a very young age and only grows more complex as we get older. Just like any other important relationship in our lives, our relationship with money is layered, emotional and sometimes complicated.

During my years of working with clients and working on myself, I came to realise that some of my mindset and some of my habits around money were deeply unhealthy. On the surface, I was always what you would call 'good with money' — a budgeter from a young age, someone who set big financial goals, someone who (at least from the outside) looked like they had their money completely under control. People assumed that because I was responsible with money, I must have had a good relationship with it. But being 'good with money' doesn't necessarily mean having *healthy* habits.

My habits weren't driven by confidence or security. They were driven by fear.

Working in finance, I saw two types of people: those who were in control of their money and those who were struggling. I was inspired by the first group and terrified of being in the second group. That fear shaped many of my financial decisions, just like it does everyone else.

A healthy relationship with money mirrors the principles of a healthy personal relationship: It's built on trust, respect and accountability. It's about treating money with care and intention, not fear or neglect. This relationship requires honesty with yourself about your financial habits, clear boundaries for spending and saving, and taking ownership of your financial decisions. It's about aligning your financial choices with your values, respecting the balance between saving for the future and enjoying the present. Most importantly, it's about ensuring that your finances serve you and empower your goals, rather than control or overwhelm you.

Creating (and maintaining) this kind of relationship with money is vital for achieving peace of mind, stability and the freedom to live a life aligned with your aspirations. Building a healthy relationship in any area of life doesn't come all that easy to a lot of us. Money is no different.

For many of us, money is tied to something even deeper: our sense of safety and self-worth. Often, these connections run so deep that we don't even realise they're there.

Money can also be a source of shame. It's not something many people feel comfortable talking about openly, which only makes it harder to address financial challenges when they arise. It's no wonder that when life throws us a major plot twist — a divorce, a job loss or any other significant change — money can feel like one of the most destabilising factors, leaving us uncertain and vulnerable.

If that's how you're feeling right now, remember: You're not alone, and it's okay to acknowledge how heavy the load feels.

As life unfolds, our relationship with money gets tangled up with emotions, shaped by childhood experiences, societal expectations and personal setbacks. It can amplify anxiety, strain relationships and even affect our physical health. That's why working on your relationship with money isn't just about the numbers; it's about finding stability and purpose in your financial life.

Your money mindset — the way you think, feel and act with money — is one of the most important factors in your financial journey. Money is about what those numbers represent: freedom, security, control and, most importantly, options.

Managing money isn't an innate skill. It's something you learn, and it's something you can get better at over time. If you're thinking, *It's too late for me to figure this out*, let me stop you right there. It's never too late. Whether you're 18 or 80, there's always room to grow, shift your perspective and build habits that serve you.

Remember, money is just a tool — a resource used to meet your needs and reach your goals. It's a learned skill, no matter your age!

What's your money story?

Your money mindset is the set of beliefs, attitudes and habits you've developed about money over time, and you'll often hear it referred to as your 'money story'. It's the result of every experience you've had, every lesson you've learned (or lack thereof) and the messages you've absorbed about money throughout your life.

Think of your money story like the lens through which you view every financial decision. It's not just a background influence — it's the script running in your mind that shapes:

- how you approach spending and saving

- whether you feel confident or anxious about money

- how you set financial goals (or avoid them entirely)

- the way you recover from setbacks and navigate financial challenges.

Your money story impacts *every* financial decision you make, often without you even realising it. It can either hold you back or propel you forward.

When your mindset is positive and empowering, you feel confident in your ability to make decisions, handle challenges and create a secure financial future. You're able to set meaningful goals and take action towards achieving them. But when your mindset is negative or limiting, it can feel like an invisible barrier, keeping you stuck in patterns that no longer serve you. It's not just about what you believe; it's about how those beliefs influence your actions. Your money mindset can become a stronghold, shaping your choices in ways that impact your ability to function, grow and move forward.

For example, if your story is rooted in scarcity, maybe you grew up hearing things like, 'Money doesn't grow on trees' or 'We can't afford that'. You might approach money with fear or anxiety. Even when you have enough, you may constantly feel like there isn't enough. This mindset can make you hesitant to invest in yourself, take calculated risks or spend on things that genuinely add value to your life.

On the other hand, if your story leans towards overindulgence, perhaps shaped by beliefs like, 'You only live once' or 'Treat yourself, you deserve it', you might find yourself overspending, even at the expense of your long-term goals. You may struggle to save consistently or feel in control of your finances because the pull to spend feels stronger than the desire to plan ahead.

In both cases, your money story can become a self-fulfilling prophecy.

See money as scarce? You'll avoid taking opportunities to grow your wealth, reinforcing the feeling of scarcity.

See money as something to spend freely? You might end up in cycles of financial stress, reinforcing the idea that you can't get ahead.

Your money story can make you second-guess yourself, avoid necessary financial conversations or feel paralysed when faced with important decisions. For many people, a limiting money story holds them back from:

- asking for a raise or negotiating their salary
- investing in personal or professional growth
- addressing debt because it feels overwhelming or shameful
- setting realistic financial goals because they fear failure or doubt their ability to succeed.

In its most extreme forms, a negative money story can lead to avoidance: ignoring bank statements, putting off retirement planning or delaying important decisions because facing your finances feels too overwhelming. This avoidance doesn't just affect your financial health. It can spill over into your mental health, relationships and overall quality of life. We'll dive into some common patterns shortly, but for now, just know there is good news here.

The good news is that recognising your mindset is the first step towards reshaping it.

Once you understand the story you've been telling yourself, you can decide to rewrite it in a way that aligns with your values and goals.

Reset now: Determine your money mindset

Like any transformation, the starting point is always reflection. To start uncovering your money story, reflect on the following questions and make some notes.

What did I learn about money growing up?

What phrases or lessons about money did I hear from those closest to me?

_____

_____

How was money handled in my family? Was it a source of stress, secrecy or opportunity?

_____

_____

What emotions do I associate with money?

Do I feel anxious, confident or guilty when I think about my finances?

_____

_____

What triggers these emotions?

_____

_____

How do I view people with money?

Do I see wealth as a positive or negative thing?

_____

_____

Do I believe people with money worked hard for it, or do I feel resentful towards them?

_____

_____

What habits or patterns do I notice in myself?

Do I avoid looking at my bank account or overspend when I'm stressed?

_____

_____

Do I save compulsively, even at the expense of enjoying life?

_____

_____

Reflect on the notes you've made. What did you discover about yourself and your own money story? Did any of your answers surprise you?

_____

_____

_____

_____

_____

Beliefs → behaviours → outcomes

As you reflect on your answers to these questions, you might notice a common thread: the beliefs you hold about money. These beliefs are powerful. They create behaviours, and those behaviours, in turn, create outcomes. Whether those outcomes are helpful or harmful, it all begins with the underlying belief.

Let's break it down into a simple cycle:

Belief: The story you tell yourself about money, whether you're aware of it or not.

Behaviour: The actions and habits that stem from that belief.

Outcome: The results those behaviours produce, which often reinforce the original belief.

For example:

Belief: I'll always be in debt; it's normal.

Behaviour: You avoid budgeting, ignore your bank account or only make minimum payments.

Outcome: Your debt grows and, with it, the belief that getting out of debt is impossible.

This cycle can either work for you or against you — it all depends on the beliefs driving it. The good news is, beliefs aren't set in stone. With awareness and intention, you can challenge and rewrite them.

Imagine flipping the above script:

Belief: I can take small steps to get out of debt.

Behaviour: You create a budget, cut unnecessary expenses and make consistent extra repayments.

Outcome: Your debt decreases, you feel more in control and your belief shifts to 'I *can* do this.'

Reset now: Assess your beliefs

Think about a financial belief that's been shaping your actions, whether it's about debt, saving, investing or your ability to manage money. What story have you been telling yourself?

Complete these sentences.

Right now, I believe:

_____

_____

Now, challenge it. If that belief were flipped into something more empowering, what would it look like?

Instead, I choose to believe:

_____

_____

With this new belief, what actions would support it? What's one small, consistent step you could take?

The action I will take is:

_____

_____

What will change when you follow through? How will your financial situation (and confidence) improve?

When I take action, the outcome will be:

_____

_____

This is your chance to take control of the cycle. Are your current beliefs helping you move forward or are they keeping you stuck? You get to decide the story you tell yourself, so make it one that works in your favour.

Who's running the money mindset show?

Your approach to money might be shaped by elements of scarcity, abundance, survival, avoidance, status, security or generosity. Most of us have a mix of these but, usually, one dominant perspective runs the show.

Recognising which mindset drives your financial decisions is a crucial step towards understanding your relationship with money and, ultimately, reshaping it.

Let's look at some of the most common money mindsets that may be on repeat in your brain, so we can then explore how they influence your financial habits, decisions and outcomes.

Remember, none of the mindsets we're about to cover are inherently 'good' or 'bad'. Each has its strengths and weaknesses and, let's face it, most of us carry a mix of them at different times. The goal isn't to get rid of one mindset completely or fully embrace another. It's about finding a balance that works for *you* and supports the financial life you want to build.

Mindset 1: Scarcity

- Rooted in fear, this mindset believes there's never enough.

- People with a scarcity mindset may be overly cautious, avoid risks and feel anxious about spending.

- *Strength:* Encourages thoughtfulness and careful planning.

- *Challenge:* Can hold you back from growth and stop you from enjoying the rewards of your hard work.

Mindset 2: Abundance

- Driven by optimism and confidence in financial possibilities.
- People with an abundance mindset often focus on growth, take bold actions and pursue long-term goals.
- *Strength:* Inspires big-picture thinking and opportunities.
- *Challenge:* If unchecked, it can lead to overspending or risky decisions.

Mindset 3: Survival

- Focuses on short-term stability, prioritising immediate needs over long-term growth.
- People with a survival mindset often feel stuck in a cycle of living payday to payday.
- *Strength:* Ensures essentials are met during tough times.
- *Challenge:* Can prevent planning for the future or building wealth.

Mindset 4: Avoidance

- Driven by discomfort or anxiety around money, leading to inaction.
- People with this mindset may ignore bills, avoid budgeting or procrastinate on financial tasks.
- *Strength:* Temporary relief from stress.
- *Challenge:* Creates bigger problems and long-term instability.

Mindset 5: Status

- Views money as a way to signal success or worth.

- People with a status mindset may prioritise appearances or keeping up with others, even at the expense of their financial stability.

- *Strength:* Motivation to set ambitious financial goals.

- *Challenge:* Can lead to overspending and lack of focus on long-term security.

Mindset 6: Security

- Focused on stability, safety nets and financial preparedness.

- People with a security mindset are diligent savers who prioritise reducing risk.

- *Strength:* Provides peace of mind and strong foundations.

- *Challenge:* Can lead to missed opportunities if taken too far.

Mindset 7: Generosity

- Sees money as a tool for creating impact and helping others.

- People with a generosity mindset find joy in giving but may struggle to set boundaries.

- *Strength:* Creates meaning and connection.

- *Challenge:* Sacrificing personal financial wellbeing for others.

By recognising your dominant mindset, and how it plays a role in shaping your behaviours and decisions, you can start to see what's helping you and what's holding you back. Maybe your scarcity mindset is keeping you from taking a bold step that could lead to growth. Or perhaps your generosity mindset, while fulfilling, is making it hard to prioritise building your emergency fund or securing your future.

This isn't about flipping a switch and rewriting your money story overnight. It's about noticing the patterns that show up and asking yourself the right questions (like your sleep-at-night test questions from page 27) to guide your next move. Are these decisions aligned with your values? Do they honour your non-negotiables?

A balanced money mindset might look like:

- combining the caution of scarcity with the optimism of abundance

- saving and preparing for the future while still enjoying life today (because what's the point of all that planning if you're too burned out to enjoy the journey?)

- taking calculated risks — not avoiding them out of fear, but also not diving in recklessly without considering your sleep-at-night test

- giving generously while maintaining boundaries to protect your financial wellbeing and honour your non-negotiables.

When you approach money with a mindset that balances growth, security and self-compassion, you stop letting your subconscious run the show. Instead, you take control, making intentional decisions that not only support your financial goals but also allow you to sleep soundly at night. That's where the real transformation happens.

Reset now: Identify your money mindset

Which of these seven mindsets do you think is your dominant one? Why?

_____

_____

What can you do to balance it out more?

_____

_____

Bias and patterns

Wrapped up with your overall money mindset are two key pieces to the financial puzzle: *biases* and *patterns*. These are the mental shortcuts and habits that influence your financial decisions, often without you even realising it.

Biases are the brain's way of processing information quickly. But if we're not careful, these mental shortcuts can quietly steer us in the wrong direction. There are countless biases out there, and understanding how they work can be a game changer. Recognising them gives you the power to pause, reflect and make more intentional choices.

Let's break down a few common ones:

- *Present bias:* This is the tendency to prioritise today's wants over tomorrow's needs. It's the YOLO (you only live once) mindset — indulging in impulse buys like new shoes, the latest iPhone or a fancy dinner, even when it means putting off savings or long-term goals. It feels great in the moment but often leads to regret later when the bills are due.

- *Confirmation bias:* This is the classic tendency to seek out information that supports what you already believe while ignoring anything that contradicts it. For example, if you're convinced an investment is a sure thing, you might focus on glowing reviews while dismissing warnings. This overconfidence can lead to risky decisions that don't align with your goals.

- *Herding bias:* The 'everyone else is doing it, so it must be a good idea' mentality. Whether it's jumping on a trendy investment or buying the latest gadget, following the crowd can leave you stuck with choices that don't truly serve you or your financial future.

In my two decades of working with people and their finances, I've seen these biases play out time and time again. And here's the thing: Biases like these don't disappear. They're hardwired into how our brains work. But the goal isn't to eliminate them; it's to *recognise* them. Yes, we can eventually rewrite them, but it will take time. When you recognise them, you create space to pause, reflect and make decisions that align with your values and goals instead of reacting on autopilot.

Which of these patterns sound familiar to you?

Stop-start: repeat

This is me with fitness goals. You have bursts of intense focus (saving diligently, for example) followed by neglect when life gets busy.

Tip to break it: Prioritise consistency. Start small, automate your savings and make steady progress a habit.

Panic response

Only dealing with finances in a crisis, then going back to ignoring them once the panic subsides.

Tip to break it: Schedule regular financial check-ins *before* a crisis hits. Build resilience by staying ahead of your money, even when things are calm.

Self-sabotage

Undermining progress because of limiting beliefs like, 'I'm just not good with money' or 'I'll never get ahead.'

Tip to break it: Challenge these beliefs. Write them down, question their validity and replace them with more empowering statements like we did in the exercise on page 41. Tools like journaling or working with a coach can help.

Avoidance

Ignoring finances out of fear or overwhelm — like not opening bills or avoiding your bank account after a spending blowout.

Tip to break it: Take small, manageable steps. Set a specific time to review your finances regularly, even for just 15 minutes.

Comparison

Feeling inadequate because you're comparing your finances to others', especially on social media.

Tip to break it: Focus on *your* goals and values. Practise gratitude, and remember that social media is a highlight reel, not real life.

Instant gratification

Prioritising short-term pleasures over long-term goals; spending now instead of saving for what truly matters.

Tip to break it: Practise delayed gratification. Set savings targets, remove temptations like credit cards from your phone, and introduce a rule where you wait 24 to 48 hours before making purchases (chances are you might realise you don't really need/ want the item).

Reset now: Identify bias and patterns

What's one financial habit or decision you've made recently that might have been influenced by bias?

_____

_____

_____

Which of the six patterns feels familiar to you in how you might have reacted?

_____

_____

_____

(continued)

What might you do differently next time you notice that mindset playing out?

_____

_____

_____

_____

What habits are holding you back?

There are patterns we can identify with reflection — ones we know are holding us back — but there are also habits that, on the surface, seem like good money moves but are quietly doing more harm than good.

Sometimes, what feels like a smart financial decision can actually create bigger challenges. It's easy to assume you're making the 'right' choices, but even seemingly healthy behaviours can have unintended consequences. These 'good' habits might be holding you back.

Do any of the following sound familiar?

- You set a savings goal and automate deposits each pay, but you're constantly dipping into your savings because you run out of cash before the next pay.

- You've automated payments but they constantly bounce because there isn't enough money in that account on the day they are scheduled.

- You pay extra on your home loan but end up relying on credit cards or buy-now-pay-later services for everyday expenses.

- You use one offset account for all of your money, which helps reduce the interest on your home loan, but you have no transparency over what money is for bills or what is for savings, and you end up overspending each month.

If you are in a cycle of one step forward, two steps back, not only are you not getting ahead, but you're reinforcing negative beliefs like, 'I'm just not good with money'.

Your systems should work for you, not against you. Just like breaking patterns starts with awareness, you can change your financial outcomes by designing systems that align with your deeply ingrained money traits. The habits and behaviours that have shaped your financial decisions have developed over years. Instead of trying to rewrite them all at once, focus on recognising what's holding you back and creating systems to minimise their impact.

When we dive into earning income and managing your spending, we'll explore practical systems like bank account structures, methods to curb overspending, and other tools that can help counteract any unproductive habits you've picked up along the way.

Reset now: Challenge your habits

What's one money habit you've always considered 'smart' but might actually be making things harder for you?

_____

_____

Remember this

Improving your relationship with money takes time, effort and a fair bit of discomfort. It's tempting to put it off until later, but ignoring it only makes things harder down the line.

Changing your relationship with money takes three key elements:

- *Awareness:* Recognise what (beliefs, biases and habits) is driving your decisions.

- *Challenge:* Ask yourself, *Are these helping me or holding me back?*

- *Action:* Small, consistent steps break the cycle. Big changes don't happen overnight, but progress builds momentum and momentum builds confidence.

While you're progressively changing your mindset, addressing biases and breaking old patterns, having the right systems in place can make the entire process much easier. Habits, especially those deep-seated ones tied to your money story, take time to change. Building new, healthier habits requires effort and consistency — and the right systems act like safety rails to keep you on track while you're doing the work.

You can have the best financial plan in the world, but without systems to support your daily habits, it's likely to fail. It's not enough to simply *want* to make better financial choices. You need practical systems that make it easier to follow through, even on the days you're tired, stressed or tempted to fall back into old patterns. James Clear sums it up perfectly in *Atomic Habits*: 'You do not rise to the level of your goals. You fall to the level of your systems.' (We'll look more at this in Chapter 5.)

Reset now: Pay attention to money moments

Over the next four weeks (ideally longer, but no less than four weeks), start paying attention to how you feel about money in everyday moments. Make it as simple as you need: a piece of paper on the fridge where you'll see it daily, notes in your phone or even a calendar reminder to check in with yourself.

Each time you interact with money, whether it's paying a bill, making a purchase or checking your bank account, write down:

1. What happened? A bill arrived, you made a purchase, you saved money, you avoided looking at your bank balance — whatever it was, jot it down.

2. How did you feel in that moment? Confident? Stressed? Guilty? In control? Notice the emotions.

3. What was your thought process? Did a bias or habit influence your choice, or was it a rational decision?

By tracking these moments, you'll start to see patterns in your emotions and decision-making. This awareness is the first step to transforming your relationship with money — because when you recognise the patterns, you gain the power to change them.

Chapter 4

Resetting your goals

Years ago, I worked with a client who came to me after a financial setback that left her feeling completely lost. She wasn't drowning in debt, but she wasn't moving forward either. She described her life as 'treading water', barely staying afloat and never making progress. When I asked her what her financial goals were, she paused, then admitted, 'Honestly? I don't know. I've just been trying to survive.'

And she isn't alone. Without goals, it's easy to fall into the daily grind, moving through life on autopilot and later wondering, *What did I actually accomplish? Where did all that money go?*

Goals act as a compass, providing direction and purpose when the path ahead feels unclear. They remind us that the small, everyday decisions we make (like choosing to save instead of spend or saying no to an impulse buy) are part of a bigger picture. They help us focus not just on where we are, but on where we *want to go.*

When things feel chaotic or uncertain, your goals remind you that this tough moment is just that — a moment. It's temporary, and you're working towards something bigger.

Think about it. How many times have you felt stuck or overwhelmed, only to feel a shift when you started focusing on what you *want* instead of what's going wrong? Goals do that. They give you something to hold onto, something to spark excitement and make the hard work feel worth it.

But it's not just about having *any* goals; it's about having the *right* goals. Goals that align with your values, your priorities and the life you want to create.

In my experience working with all kinds of clients, when you ask most people about their goals, they often default to career or work-related aspirations. Their sense of self is often tied to professional achievements, leaving personal and financial goals as an afterthought. The issue with tying goals solely to work? It often overlooks our deeper *why* — what we truly want, what brings us happiness and fulfilment.

I learned this firsthand when my ex-husband finished work before he had even turned 40 because of his health. We assumed it would solve everything — less pain, better health management, more time with the kids, and him being home more would mean I could focus on my career. Financially, we were secure thanks to the right insurance (more on that in Chapter 10), but what we didn't anticipate was the psychological toll — his loss of identity.

It was an adjustment I had naively overlooked. I'd helped clients navigate this transition after 40 years of work and I had seen their challenges, yet for some reason, I saw his situation differently. Work wasn't his whole life — he had his family, hobbies and friends — so I assumed he'd simply have *more* time for those.

But in reality, the challenges were strikingly similar to those of a retiree at 65. I just hadn't seen it coming.

When it comes to goal setting for the new you, the key is ensuring your goals reflect you — not just your career, but your values, passions and the life you truly want to live.

Start with values

Losing your job, going through a breakup, facing a major life shift — there's no denying how tough these moments can be. Let's not downplay that. They can bring uncertainty, grief and a sense of being completely unmoored. But, in time, they can also create space for reflection, offering an opportunity to realign with what truly matters to you.

Core values are the deeply held beliefs and principles that shape your decisions, guide your behaviours and influence how you define success. They help you prioritise what truly matters across relationships, career, finances and beyond. And when life forces a reset, they become even more important.

Once you've begun shifting your money mindset, the next step in transforming your financial life (and, let's be honest, your whole life) is uncovering your 'why'. This is the driving force behind your choices and goals. It's what gives you the motivation to keep going, even on the hard days.

Your 'why' or core values are the things that matter most to you. They become your anchor, giving purpose and direction to your financial goals.

Rediscovering them helps you cut through external pressures and expectations so that the choices you make moving forward are truly your own, and not shaped by what your ex-partner thought, what your best friend is doing or what someone else says you 'should' prioritise. This clarity is essential when rebuilding and setting new goals that feel meaningful and aligned with who you are now.

Reconnecting with your values can feel like peeling back layers of your identity. So much of who we are gets wrapped up in career, financial stability and life roles, and when those things shift, it's normal to feel unsettled. But it's also an opportunity to redefine what really matters to you.

Some examples of core values that might resonate with you are:

Freedom: The ability to make choices and live life on your terms.

Family: Nurturing relationships and creating a sense of belonging.

Security: Feeling stable and protected, especially financially.

Growth: Constantly learning, improving and challenging yourself.

Contribution: Making a difference in the lives of others or your community.

Discovering, or rediscovering, your core values involves introspection and self-reflection.

Follow these four simple steps to begin.

Reflect on peak moments: Think about times when you felt most fulfilled, happy or proud. What were you doing? Who were you with? What values were being honoured?

Consider what upsets you: Often, what frustrates or upsets you can reveal your core values. If dishonesty deeply bothers you, integrity might be a core value.

Examine past decisions: Look at significant choices you've made, both good and bad. What values guided those decisions?

List and prioritise: Write down potential values and narrow the list to a few core ones. These will become the guiding principles for your life and financial decisions.

Reset now: Reassess your values

Use the following four steps to write out the three to five guiding values you will take into every financial decision you now make.

1. Reflect on key moments.

2. Consider what upsets you.

3. Examine past decisions.

4. List and prioritise your values.

Your guiding values in order:

1. _____

2. _____

3. _____

4. _____

5. _____

Aligning your values with new goals

Core values (those deeply held beliefs that guide your decisions) are the foundation of meaningful goal setting. When your goals align with your values, every step feels more natural and purposeful.

The right goals resonate with your core values and reflect the life you want to create. When your goals align with what matters to you, they're more motivating, more fulfilling and far easier to stick with when things get tough.

Here's how that alignment might look:

- *If freedom or independence is a core value:* Your goals might focus on building income-producing assets, such as investments or a side hustle, that allow you to control your time and choices.

- *If family is central to your life:* You might prioritise saving for your children's education or creating a work-life balance that allows for quality time with loved ones.

- *If personal growth drives you:* Your goals could involve investing in education, career development or experiences that challenge you.

On the flip side, when there's a disconnect between your values and your financial habits, it often shows up as feelings of stress, dissatisfaction or that awful, stuck-in-a-rut sensation.

For example:

- You value freedom, but your spending habits keep you tied to debt, limiting your options.

- You value family, but work commitments mean you're missing important milestones with your kids.

- You value growth, but you're too afraid to invest in yourself, leaving you feeling stagnant.

Often, our goals can become tunnel-visioned, driven by societal norms or outdated assumptions. For example, not so long ago, I realised I'd been approaching life like a checklist of what I thought success should look like: the job, the engagement, the house, the kids, the next career move. It all felt like a natural progression, but I hadn't stopped to question why that version of success mattered to me.

It's not that those milestones didn't bring happiness — they absolutely did, and still do. But when I reflected, I realised I was following a script I hadn't consciously written, going through the motions without intention. What's wrong with having a checklist of 'success'? Nothing really, until a plot twist comes along.

Divorce wasn't on the list, and when the checklist derailed, it left me feeling lost, and as though I'd failed.

The problem isn't the milestones themselves; it's tying your sense of worth to a rigid list that doesn't allow for these detours (or maybe road closures is a more accurate term).

To get clear on whether the goals you think are your goals are truly yours, you need to challenge them. Take the time to understand the driving force behind them and how they align with your values.

For example, a common goal I often see is home ownership, with the first milestone being saving for a deposit. While it's a great goal for many, I'm finding more and more often that it doesn't always align with a person's true values. Instead, it often stems from societal expectations or the belief that it's simply what you're 'supposed to do'.

If home ownership is a goal of yours, you could ask yourself:

- What values of mine does owning a home align with?

- Does this make sense in terms of what I envision for my life?

- Do I plan to live in one place long-term, or am I more of a nomad?

- Could I see myself living overseas or retiring somewhere entirely different?

- How will owning a home feel?

- Will I sleep better at night if I own my own home and why?

If your core value is freedom and flexibility, buying a home to live in might not align with your vision — especially if you plan to travel or relocate frequently. In that case, you could be exploring other financial decisions that build wealth while supporting your values. Now that might still be property, but maybe it's not a home you live in. There are multiple ways you can meet a need or a value you hold without taking the traditional path.

At different times in your life, there are going to be moments when things just don't align — the work commitments example is a common one. It's all well and good to say 'Cut back on work to spend more time with family because that's a value', but in your reality, that might not be an option... yet. If it doesn't feel like an option right now, it doesn't mean it can't be a goal you're working towards. The key here is knowing your values and setting goals around them so you have a clear sense of where you're heading and why it matters to you.

Recognising these misalignments is an important step to creating goals that feel authentic and fulfilling. This alignment not only makes the journey more rewarding but ensures that when you reach your goals, they'll actually feel meaningful.

Keep this in mind as we head into the next step and set new goals.

When your goals reflect your values, every decision you make becomes a step towards the life you genuinely want — not the one you think you should have.

Are there any goals that you've set that are out of alignment with who you really are?

Jot these down now.

_____

_____

_____

_____

_____

Setting goals for the new you

I often see people going through tough life changes struggle to set goals for their future selves. Sometimes it's because they're overthinking it, feeling like their goals need to be massive leaps forward — but they don't.

Maybe your goal is something as simple as:

- not stressing about bills
- avoiding overdrawn fees
- reviewing your subscriptions and cancelling the unused ones
- finally tackling something you've been putting off.

Or maybe your goal is as big as achieving ultimate financial independence — a target of the amount of wealth you aspire to achieve.

Wherever you're starting from, remember: You have to walk before you run. Small goals create momentum, and that momentum shows you that change is possible. Every small step is a step forward.

Your goals are *yours*. They don't have to be big, audacious or impressive to anyone else — they just need to make sense to you and where you are right now. If you're ready to start setting goals that align with your values and reflect the positive mindset you want to embody, start with these steps.

Reflect on where you've been

Before setting new goals, take some time to reflect on your past. This isn't about dwelling on mistakes; it's about learning from them to create a better future. Reflection helps you understand what has shaped your current circumstances and what lessons you want to carry forward (or leave behind). Ask yourself:

- *What has worked?* Identify the strategies, habits or behaviours that have helped you succeed in the past. These are your strengths: tools you can use again.

- *What hasn't worked?* Be honest about the patterns or approaches that haven't served you.

- *What might not serve you any more?* Life evolves, and so do your needs and priorities. What worked five years ago might not be effective today.

Reflection isn't a one-time task. It's an ongoing process. Be brutally honest with yourself but also compassionate. Maybe you regret putting that European holiday on credit years ago, but beating yourself up over it won't change anything. When we know better, we do better — and now you know better (or at least you will by the end of this book).

Start with your values

Let the core values you identified on page 59 guide your goals. By reflecting on where you've been and identifying what truly matters moving forward, you'll create goals that align with your authentic self.

Remember: your values are the *why* behind your actions — your deeper motivations and guiding principles. A strategy, on the other hand, is the *how* — the specific plans or methods to bring those values to life.

For example, your goal might be to build an emergency fund. But ask yourself *why*. Is it because you want to feel secure knowing you can cover unexpected expenses? Or maybe it's about feeling stable enough to handle a job loss or emergency without financial stress.

Be specific

Vague goals lead to vague outcomes. Instead of saying, 'I want to build an emergency fund', say, 'I want to save $10 000 for an emergency fund within 12 months'. Clear, measurable targets give you direction and make it easier to track progress.

Make sure you write them down somewhere you'll see them every day. Keeping your goals visible keeps them top of mind and boosts your motivation to stick with them.

Break down big goals

Big goals can feel overwhelming. Break them into smaller, actionable steps. For example: if your goal is to save $10 000 in 12 months, ask yourself:

- What does that look like each payday?
- Will you save a fixed amount each pay?
- Will you set smaller milestones, like reaching $1000, $2500 and so on?

Breaking down big goals into manageable chunks makes them feel achievable and keeps you motivated. Have a go at making them meaningful milestones.

If your savings goal is $20 000, skipping a $20 breakfast on the run or a $50 car detail might not feel like it makes a dent. But if your milestone is $1000, suddenly every $20 or $50 saved feels much more significant.

Set milestones at amounts that make those little day-to-day savings feel impactful. This way, every extra dollar saved or earned feels like a meaningful step forward. Those small wins will keep you motivated and steadily moving towards your larger goal.

Write them on your bathroom mirror, set them as your phone or laptop screensaver or, like me, print them out as a vision board. However, you do it, the key is having a reminder of what you're working towards.

Staying motivated on your financial journey isn't just about setting goals. It's about keeping them visible and front of mind.

Vision and vision boards

For me, after my divorce, I had no idea what my future looked like. Everything felt uncertain, and for the first time in what felt like forever, I did not have clear financial goals or clear anything goals for that matter. This was pretty unnerving for someone who plans out every aspect of their lives and who loves a checklist and an over-the-top spreadsheet.

While I couldn't put my finger on clear goals, I did have a phrase that kept circling in my head that became my anchor. That phrase was and still is: 'I'm building a life beyond my wildest dreams.'

The power in that phrase was the word beyond — it gave me hope that life could get not just better, but better than I could even imagine. Even when I couldn't picture the details, I held onto the idea that something extraordinary was out there waiting for me. Something I couldn't even dream up just yet.

When it came to creating my vision board (something my friends had endlessly encouraged until I finally caved), it felt a little forced at first. As a spreadsheet person, this was completely outside my comfort zone. I'd start, leave it, come back, tweak it — until it finally clicked. If I was building a life beyond my wildest dreams, what were the things that would help me get there?

I realised that no matter what my future looked like, it had to be built around three key elements: happier, healthier, wealthier.

After all, I knew I had to become happier, I knew I wanted to be healthier, and I knew the life I was creating will need me to be wealthier.

So my vision board took shape with those three sections:

- *Happier:* Photos of my kids, my friends, travel.
- *Healthier:* Tennis, hiking, the beach — reminders to move my body and look after my wellbeing.
- *Wealthier:* A beautiful home I'd love to own, images that reflect financial safety and security, and small money habits that make a difference.

At the centre, I placed one simple question:

- What did you do today to be happier, healthier and wealthier?

Some days, the actions were tiny, but they still counted:

- *Happier:* Laughing out loud at a silly story, taking ten minutes to enjoy a cuppa in the sun instead of rushing back to my desk.
- *Healthier:* A short walk (even if it was just past the shops for a little treat), adding extra veggies to my dinner.
- *Wealthier:* Making breakfast at home instead of grabbing something on the go, finding a discount code before ordering takeaway.

That vision board is still with me. It's my laptop screensaver and it's pinned on the wall inside my wardrobe where I see it every morning and every night. It's a constant reminder that, while I have big goals, some days just getting through the day is an achievement in itself and, on those days, my goal is simple: to do one thing (no matter how small) that enriches my life today and sets me up for tomorrow. And I know that future me will also prioritise being happier, healthier and wealthier so it was the perfect combo for me.

Even my kids have started getting involved. They're at an age where they understand what it means to be happier, healthier and wealthier, and how important it is to make choices that serve us now and in the future. It's become a shared practice that we talk about each day, a new part of our day that I always look forward to.

But that doesn't have to be your approach. Maybe you find joy in a mind map or checklist on a spreadsheet. Perhaps you're someone who jots down ideas and dreams on the back of a napkin during a coffee break, or maybe you prefer the reflective process of journaling. For some, a Pinterest board filled with inspiration or a folder on your phone with photos and quotes that remind you of the life you're working towards feels more personal.

The method doesn't matter. What's important is finding a way to keep your future life in your sights.

Celebrate your wins!

Every win, no matter how small, deserves recognition. Celebrating progress keeps you motivated and makes the journey more enjoyable. Just keep it in line with your financial goals — so maybe skip the blowout shopping spree or that spontaneous Europe trip (as tempting as it might be!).

Celebrations don't have to be big or expensive. If you're anything like me, the satisfaction of ticking something off a to-do list or updating your spreadsheet might be enough. But if that's not your style, find what feels like a meaningful reward to you. Maybe it's treating yourself to a nice coffee, taking a slow morning off or sharing your success with someone who is in your village — maybe your accountability partner or cheerleader?

Reset now: Celebrate!

Take a moment to list five ways you can reward yourself for reaching financial milestones — big or small. Choose things that genuinely add value to your life (for example, a massage, coffee with a friend or going to the movies with the family) and keep you motivated along the way.

1. _____

2. _____

3. _____

4. _____

5. _____

Who in your village will you share your wins with?

_____

_____

It's okay to let go

When I went through my own reset, I found that some of the financial goals I had clung to, things that I thought were of the utmost importance to me (like owning a home to live in or sailing around Australia when I can't sail or even drive a boat and have no intention to learn) no longer fit my new reality. What once seemed like the ultimate endgame no longer aligned with who I was becoming. Now this doesn't mean they are off the table forever, but right now, a lot of old goals seem very out of reach and, honestly, not important.

Accepting it's okay to let go can be both liberating and challenging. It requires a significant shift in perspective and a readiness to redefine what success and fulfilment mean for you. It's not about lowering your expectations or settling for less. It's about ensuring your goals are genuinely yours — authentic and aligned with your current reality and values.

If you go through this process and come out with the same goals — congratulations, that's fantastic! If your goals change, that's perfectly okay too. Letting go of outdated ambitions creates space for growth, resilience and a future that's not just about ticking boxes but about living a life filled with purpose, fulfilment and joy.

Shift your focus to what you'll gain, not what you're leaving behind.

This perspective makes all the difference in embracing change and moving forward with confidence.

Letting go of the family home I shared with my ex was one of the hardest decisions I've ever had to make. Like the decision to end my marriage, it didn't come out of nowhere. I'd thought about it for a long time, which gave me time to consider the practical and emotional side of things, because, like most decisions, it was never just about the financial numbers on paper. This decision was tied to so much more.

First and foremost, I wanted stability for our children. They had lived in that house their whole lives, and in the middle of all the upheaval, it felt like the one constant I could try to protect. Then there was my ex. Ending a marriage is hard enough, and the last thing I wanted was to uproot every aspect of his life. He loved (loves) that house as I did. We had painstakingly turned that house into our dream home with years of hard work, and I knew he would fight to keep it. I didn't want to add more conflict to an already painful situation.

Plus, deep down, I knew I didn't have the time, energy or desire to manage the house on my own. Between the ongoing maintenance and list of half-done DIY projects we had started (okay, mostly *I* had started) and never finished, the thought of taking it all on felt overwhelming.

After many sleepless nights and countless 'what if' scenarios, I came to a realisation that ultimately felt right: Although I absolutely loved that house, I knew I could live anywhere and make it feel like home. At the time, though, I still assumed I would end up in another house I owned — just not *that* house. Renting long-term wasn't even on my radar. (Yet here I am currently renting long-term.)

What I hadn't anticipated in making that decision and a lot of others, was how much of my self-worth was tied to my perception of financial success, and how, for me, financial success meant owning the home I lived in. After all, it was on my invisible success checklist. Letting go of that belief was far harder than I imagined. Initially, there was a heavy sense of financial failure.

Even after settling into my new, low-maintenance rental (a place I've grown to genuinely love and feel so settled), those thoughts resurface. I catch myself wondering if I should revisit the dream of owning a home — after all, all my friends are living in homes they own, paying off their own mortgages. But when I pause to reflect on my current goals and the life I'm creating for myself and my children, I remind myself that this longing often stems from my outdated goals and values — ones shaped by a different version of me, living a completely different chapter of life.

Letting go of the family home — and the dream of owning the home I live in, at least for now — has opened the door for me to pursue goals that genuinely matter to me today. And that's what this process is all about: checking in with yourself, recognising what no longer serves you and making room for the life you truly want to create.

That doesn't mean I won't own a home again in the future, but right now, it doesn't align with who I am or what I want and the other financial strategies that I'm utilising to create my own financial safety and security.

Remember, the only path that truly matters is the one that feels right for you (and, yes, you are allowed to second-guess yourself along the way). Flexibility is key. Goals aren't set in stone; they're a guide to help you move forward. As your life evolves, so should your goals.

Life is unpredictable, circumstances change, and your goals may need to adapt. Regularly reassess and adjust your goals to ensure they stay relevant and aligned with your values.

Your money reset is about taking control of the practical side of your finances. It's about challenging old habits, reassessing the way money flows in and out of your life and making sure your financial setup truly supports the future you're working. The way you managed money before might not work for where you're headed now — and that's okay.

Next up: getting real with your budget. Let's make sure your money is working for you, not the other way around.

Chapter 5

Budgeting for the new you

A client of mine, Sarah, first came to me after a sudden divorce in her late 40s. It's a fairly common scenario I see. She'd spent years as the primary caregiver, working part-time on and off, and most of the household expenses were being covered by her working partner.

Suddenly, she was on her own, overwhelmed by bills, unsure how to make ends meet and terrified about what her financial future would look like. Like a lot of the people I see, her ex had defaulted to the primary money-manager role, and she'd defaulted to the primary parent role. It was all working great while they were together, but after separating, Sarah had expenses she now needed to cover and was feeling completely out of her depth.

When we sat down to figure out her next steps, I could see how paralysed she felt. She kept saying, 'I don't even know where to start'. And honestly, that's how most people feel after life pulls the rug out from under them.

No matter your age, stage of life or how overwhelming the situation may seem, there are always things that are within your control to help improve your financial position.

Your levers

Levers are the actions you can take to shift your financial situation. They're the tools at your disposal that, when pulled intentionally, create meaningful change.

The two most common levers are:

- *Spending less:* Identify areas where you can cut costs or reduce unnecessary expenses to create more breathing room in your budget; create a surplus that means you can smash your goals and build wealth.

- *Earning more:* Find ways to boost your income so you have more money to cover expenses, achieve your goals, save or invest. (We'll delve into this one in more detail in Chapter 6.)

Sarah didn't need to overhaul everything overnight. She just needed to figure out what, and when, to pull in each lever to start building momentum and start making some changes.

Sometimes these levers, especially if it means spending less, can feel like a setback. And, yes, they may mean sacrifices now, but let's reframe these — they are actually 'slingshot moments'.

Imagine pulling back a slingshot: You create tension, step back and feel the resistance. That pullback isn't permanent; it's building momentum. When you release, you don't just return to where you were. You launch forward with even more force, often ending up in a much better position than you ever imagined!

You *will* bounce back—and when you do, you'll be propelled forward in a way that wouldn't have been possible without this moment of adjustment.

Here are some common slingshot moments.

Cutting back on discretionary spending

Skipping luxuries like dining out or taking holidays might feel restrictive, but redirecting those funds can help rebuild your financial foundation or achieve a specific goal more quickly.

Downgrading your car or wardrobe

Opting for a more modest car or wardrobe can free up cash for more meaningful financial goals. Two sayings I love are 'Drive the cheapest car you can afford' and 'Don't wear or drive your wealth.'

Downsizing your home

Moving from a larger property into a smaller one might feel like a step backward, but the financial flexibility it creates can be transformative. It can help you pay off debt, build a solid savings base or fund a new chapter of your life.

Increasing work hours or taking on a second job or side hustle

Increasing the hours you work (or re-entering the workforce) might feel like a loss of freedom, but it can offer the financial boost needed to regain stability or fund new dreams. Extra work may temporarily cut into your free time, but it can speed up debt repayment, boost savings or provide the financial cushion you need for a fresh start. (More on that in Chapter 6.)

By making intentional sacrifices now, you're setting yourself up for a stronger, more stable future. Pulling back may feel hard in the moment, but the momentum it creates can propel you to a place you may not have reached otherwise. Those small, deliberate choices have the power to create a ripple effect that transforms your financial situation over time.

The key to embracing the slingshot is remembering that these difficult times are temporary. They are a means to an end, and an opportunity to set you up in a much better financial position.

From survival to intentional

We've all been there. You pop into the shops for 'just one thing' and somehow leave with a trolley full of items you never planned to buy. Or maybe it's that late-night online shopping scroll — one click and *boom*, a dopamine-fuelled purchase that feels great... until the transaction hits your bank account.

One of my personal favourites? The 'treat yourself' justification. After a tough day (or even a great one!), it's easy to convince yourself that you *deserve* that little shopping spree or a takeaway dinner. It's harmless, right? Until you add up these 'small' splurges and realise they're quietly sabotaging your financial goals, not to mention often leaving us feeling riddled with guilt.

Not all financial detours are self-inflicted. Sometimes, the numbers stop adding up for reasons *completely* out of our control. A rent increase, an unexpected medical bill or the financial fallout of a life-changing event (a divorce, job loss or family emergency) can throw even the best-laid plans off track.

The good news? Whether your spending is driven by impulse or circumstance, the solution isn't to feel guilty. It's to get *intentional*.

The key isn't just spending less. It's spending in a way that aligns with what truly matters to you. That is where a budget comes in.

When life shifts overnight, expenses can spiral, not because we're careless, but because we're in survival mode, so it's important we get back on track when we can.

The budget blues

Now, I know what you're thinking: 'Budgeting? Really? Do we have to?' And look, I get it. The word 'budget' doesn't exactly scream excitement. For many, it conjures up images of spreadsheets, penny-pinching and a life of saying no to all the things that bring joy. But hear me out: A budget isn't about restriction. It's about empowerment.

Think of a budget as a plan, a tool to help you direct your money towards the things that truly matter. It tells your money where to go, rather than wondering where it all went.

So if the word 'budget' makes you cringe, call it something else: a cashflow plan, a spending guide, a money map or even a dough diary. What matters isn't the name but what it does: It gives you clarity and control over your finances.

A budget is your safety net, your strategy and your guide all in one. Without it, how can you confidently move towards financial security or achieve those big goals?

It's not about spending less. It's about spending right.

Trust me: It's much easier to make progress when you know where your money is going.

At its core, a budget is just a list of your expenses, how much they cost and how often they occur. That's it. No fluff, no unnecessary complexity, just a clear, practical way to take control of your money.

We want your budget to tell you what your expenses are, how much are they and how often they come up.

That's it.

But like a lot of 'finance' things, there are so many options, which can make it feel more confusing than it needs to be. A quick Google search will send you down a rabbit hole of options. You'll find the Barefoot Investor championing buckets, Dave Ramsey preaching the envelope system, and others swearing by the 50/30/20 rule (50 per cent of income goes to needs, 30 per cent to wants and 20 per cent to savings or debt). Then there's zero-based budgeting, where every dollar is assigned a job; pay-yourself-first budgeting, which prioritises savings before expenses; and percentage-based budgets, tailored for freelancers with variable income.

Each approach has its own devoted following, so the key is finding the one that fits your lifestyle and financial goals.

There's no one right way to budget: What works best depends on your lifestyle, income and financial goals. But I get it. In tough times, cutting through the noise can be challenging, and even when the options are laid out clearly, deciding on the best one for you can still feel overwhelming.

So, while I encourage you to experiment and find what works for you, it's often best to start with something basic. The budget we're going to look at next is a system that I regularly see work for successful money management and will be the backbone of any budget, no matter what adaptions you make down the track.

Remember, a budget is just a plan for your money. It's about telling your money where to go instead of wondering where it went.

Create a budget for the new you

Pen and paper? Excel spreadsheet? Online budget tool? There are options!

But let's just get started with a pen and the template I have included in the activity below. You can put it into a cool spreadsheet or something a bit flasher later.

I'm going to walk you through five simple steps.

Step 1: Brain dump your expenses

Start by writing down every expense you can think of off the top of your head. Rent, mortgage, groceries, subscriptions, kids' expenses, fuel — whatever comes to mind first. Don't overthink it, just get it down.

Step 2: Cross-check with bank statements

Once you've got your list, go through your bank statements and credit card transactions from at least the last three months (the longer the better). This will fill in the gaps and show you where your money is really going, not just what you remember. This is also a good chance to get realistic. If in step 1 you've said you spend $200 a week on groceries but your bank statements say otherwise, you need to update that. It needs to be realistic, not just look good on paper.

Step 3: Catch anything you've missed

It's easy to forget about the stuff that doesn't pop up every month — until it suddenly does, and your budget cops a hit!

Some of the biggest offenders? Car maintenance. New tyres, servicing (hello, 100 000 kilometre milestone) and surprise repairs can sneak up on you if you're not prepared.

And homeowners, you *know* those little 'maintenance' purchases add up. A quick Bunnings run for one thing somehow turns into a full trolley situation. When I was a homeowner, I always aimed to keep a $1000 buffer just for those inevitable Bunnings trips, because, let's be honest, there's always *something* that needs fixing, updating or replacing.

Then there are the once-a-year budget busters: car rego, annual insurance, birthdays and Christmas (yes, it comes *every* year, and it's not just gifts: think food, travel and time off work). These can blow your budget if you don't plan ahead.

If you're worried you've missed something, there are lots of free budget templates and resources online, including at the moneysmart.gov.au website, that you can use to help jog your memory. Better to catch it now than be blindsided later!

Step 4: Work out frequencies

Now that you have your list, go through each expense and note how often it occurs: weekly, fortnightly, monthly, quarterly or annually. This step is important because it helps you see the full picture, not just what's coming out of your account this week.

Once you've done all of that, convert everything you have to a fortnightly or monthly total (whatever suits your regular pay cycle) so you can see what your life actually costs. For example:

- If you get paid monthly, divide your annual expenses by 12.

- If you get paid fortnightly, divide your annual expenses by 26.

For example:

- $1200 annual insurance bill = $100 per month or $47 per fortnight

- $750 car rego every six months = $125 per month or $58 per fortnight

- weekly groceries at $200 = roughly $870 per month or $400 per fortnight

If it doesn't work out perfectly, just round it up.

Step 5: Compare your expenses to your income

Now, look at what's coming in. Write down your total household income after tax, whether it's from your salary, business, benefits or side hustles. Compare this to your total expenses.

This is the moment of truth — it's about knowing exactly where you stand so you can make informed decisions.

My income $_____

My expenses $_____

Surplus/shortfall? $_____

If your expenses are less than your income — great! Now you know exactly how much extra you have to put into savings, investing or your goals.

If your expenses are higher than your income, it's time to make some adjustments, whether that's cutting back on things that don't align with your priorities or finding ways to increase your income.

Either way, there's always room for improvement because the more you optimise, the more financial freedom and flexibility you create for yourself.

Your budget isn't about saying no to spending—it's about making sure your money is working for you, not against you!

Reset now: Begin your budget

Now it's your turn to action those five simple budgeting steps. You can set this up in your preferred app, an Excel spreadsheet or use the template below to get a snapshot of your expenses and income.

Step 1: Brain dump your expenses

Step 2: Cross-check with your bank statements

Step 3: Catch anything you've missed

Step 4: Work out frequencies and life cost

Step 5: Compare your expenses to your income

TOTAL EXPECTED INCOME: $_____

FIXED EXPENSES	AMOUNT	FREQUENCY (MONTHLY, WEEKLY, YEARLY)	ANNUAL TOTAL
	$		$
	$		$
	$		$

FIXED EXPENSES (continued)	AMOUNT	FREQUENCY (MONTHLY, WEEKLY, YEARLY)	ANNUAL TOTAL
	$		$
	$		$
	$		$
	$		$

ANNUAL EXPENDITURE

VARIABLE EXPENSES	AMOUNT	FREQUENCY	ANNUAL TOTAL
	$		$
	$		$
	$		$
	$		$
	$		$
	$		$

DISCRETIONARY SPENDING	AMOUNT	FREQUENCY	ANNUAL TOTAL
	$		$
	$		$
	$		$
	$		$
	$		$
	$		$

TOTAL ANNUAL EXPENDITURE $_____

TOTAL INCOME − TOTAL EXPENSES = DIFFERENCE
MY SURPLUS/SHORTFALL: $_____

(continued)

> Once you have an understanding of your expenses, you can use this to work out how much you need in your emergency fund to pass your sleep-a-night test.
>
> For example, if your annual expenses are $85 000 and you want to have three months' expenses in an emergency fund:
>
> $85 000 ÷ 12 = $7083 per month x 3 months = $21 250

Optimising according to your values

So, how did your budget look?

Chances are you've got some work to do — because most people do! If there's *a little too much month at the end of your money* (aka your expenses are outpacing your income), then it's time to take a closer look at where your money is going and why.

If you're navigating some tricky financial issues in your life, then this activity is important and should be a priority, but even if you're *not* in a tight spot, reviewing and optimising your expenses is still a smart move. Every dollar you free up is a dollar that can go towards your goals, your future and building a life that truly aligns with what matters to you.

So whether you're doing this out of necessity or inspiration, making your money work harder for you is always worth it.

A lot of the time, we spend money out of habit. It's easy to keep paying for things simply because we always have — expenses we assume are necessary because they've always been there. But when was the last time you really challenged them? Do they still serve you? Do they still fit with where you're at in life?

This is your chance to take a step back and decide whether your spending reflects who you *were* or who you *are* now.

This is where needs, wants and non-negotiables come into play. Back in Chapter 2, we talked about non-negotiables — those things that make sure you sleep at night. If they have a dollar figure attached to them, they are essentials that absolutely *must* be covered in your budget, no questions asked. Rent, mortgage, groceries, utilities: these are the basics that keep your life running. Then there are wants: the things that aren't essential but bring joy. The goal isn't to eliminate wants. It's to make sure they align with what actually makes you happy, not just what marketing or impulse tells you to buy.

Spending should feel good *after* the fact, not just in the moment. That's where value-aligned spending comes in. Instead of mindlessly swiping your card, value-aligned spending is about making conscious choices. It's not about cutting everything. It's about spending on what genuinely adds value to your life. When you think about what a purchase enables (or prevents), you become more empowered to make decisions that support your future, not just your fleeting emotions.

I learned this the hard way with impulse spending. My brain is a master at convincing me a purchase is *completely necessary* and, of course, deeply aligned with my values. That skincare set? Well, *self-care is important.* That expensive kitchen gadget? *Cooking at home saves money.* That last-minute holiday deal? *Experiences over things!* But the truth is, impulse spending rarely lines up with our actual priorities. If you've ever felt a twinge of regret, frustration or even shame after a purchase, that's a good sign it wasn't really aligned with what matters most to you.

The trick isn't about never spending; it's about spending with *intention.* When you buy something, it's not just the price you're paying. It's the time and effort you spent earning that money. Thinking about purchases in terms of the hours you worked for them can help you make more mindful choices. That doesn't mean you shouldn't buy the thing, take the holiday or upgrade your car. It just means doing it *deliberately*, understanding the trade-offs and making sure it fits into your bigger financial picture.

But, let's be honest, some expenses just don't spark joy, no matter how you spin it. No one gets excited about paying council rates or electricity bills but those are here to stay so we need to make sure we have room for them and the other stuff too.

I remember hearing someone say that reframing mundane chores could make them feel less tedious: Laundry isn't just laundry; it's providing clean clothes for your family. Dishes aren't just dishes; they mean you've eaten a meal. While I can't say this has magically made me *love* folding laundry (still the worst), it has stuck with me.

That same mindset shift applies to unavoidable expenses. Paying council rates might feel like a drain, but it's also what keeps public spaces maintained, the garbage collected and infrastructure running. Your electricity bill? That's what keeps your home warm in winter, your fridge running and your nights well-lit. It doesn't mean you *have* to enjoy these payments, but reframing them can make them feel less painful.

At the same time, if an expense truly isn't bringing value to your life, it might be time to cut it. Trimming the fat in your budget doesn't mean giving up everything fun; it means questioning whether the money you're spending is genuinely serving you. Maybe it's a gym membership you never use, a streaming subscription you forgot about or insurance policies that no longer suit your needs. Cutting back doesn't have to feel like deprivation; it can feel like taking back control.

It's not about restriction. It's about choice, control and spending in a way that truly reflects the life you want to build.

Controlling your costs

If cutting back is the lever you need to pull right now, remember: It's a slingshot, not a life sentence. Tightening your budget is about creating momentum, not staying stuck in restriction forever.

Here's how to control some of your biggest costs in a simple and straightforward way.

Step 1: Break it down — needs versus wants

Go through the budget you created on page 84, and highlight each expense as either a

- *need:* essentials such as housing, bills, groceries, transport and debt repayments that need to be prioritised, or a

- *want:* non-essentials such as dining out, streaming services, shopping and entertainment that can go when your budget needs tightening.

Step 2: Identify what wants can go

Now it's decision time. Based on your values, goals and non-negotiables, work through your list and decide:

- What can go permanently? Unused subscriptions, impulse shopping habits or things you don't actually enjoy might be easy things to get rid of.

- What can go temporarily? Maybe dining out is off the table for a few months, but it's not forever.

- What can be cut back? If five streaming services is too much, try rotating them instead of paying for them all at once.

- What can be swapped for free or low-cost alternatives?

Some examples might be:

- *Fake-out dinners:* Re-create the restaurant experience at home with candles, themed meals or a new recipe.

- *Free fun with friends:* Swap expensive outings for game nights, hikes or free local events.

- *Creative adventures:* Explore budget-friendly hobbies such as DIY projects, photography or community groups.

- *Library visits:* Borrow books, movies and even digital services for free. Many libraries also offer free workshops and events.

Step 3: Review your 'needs' expenses

Even your 'needs' can probably be trimmed. Just because something is essential doesn't mean you have to overpay for it. No more blindly letting renewals roll over: review them now and each time they're due.

- *Review insurances:* Car, home, health and pet insurance — when was the last time you checked if you were getting the best deal? Don't let 'loyalty tax' cost you hundreds.

- *Reduce utility bills:* Compare energy providers, check for discounts and see if you can lower your usage (even small changes add up).

Yes, cutting back on your needs and wants can feel like a struggle, but just remind yourself: this is temporary.

Reset Now: Reassess your needs

Pick three expenses in your 'needs' category that could be reviewed to see if you can get a better deal.

1. _____

2. _____

3. _____

Check what you're using, what you're paying and do a quick Google search to compare options. You might be surprised at what you find.

If today's not the day (we all have those days), just pick one and tackle it now. Then, set a reminder in your calendar for a specific date to review the others.

The key here? Make this a habit. A regular review (say, once a year) can save you *thousands* over time. But it's only valuable if you actually do it! So, lock it in and thank yourself later.

Make it fun!

Tap into what we've already covered: reframing your mindset, your slingshot moment, your vision board, your core values. Keeping your *why* front and centre makes it easier to focus on the bigger picture rather than what you're giving up.

Cutting all the fun out of your budget isn't realistic, but you can approach it creatively. Try a no-spend challenge, where you commit to zero discretionary spending for a set period. Or adopt the 48-hour rule before buying anything non-essential, where you wait 48 hours to see if you still really want it.

My personal favourite? Rotating expense cuts. Instead of vowing never to buy clothes again or giving up eating out forever (let's be honest, that's not going to happen), I pick one discretionary expense to cut each month. The best part? You can plan it around your social calendar: Skip takeaways during a quiet month, pause clothes shopping when there are no events on the calendar, or ditch those subscriptions you're barely using until your new show is out ready to binge in one go. Small, intentional tweaks add up over time without making life feel restrictive.

You're not just cutting back. You're creating space for something better.

A budget without baggage

I get that all of this can be hard and confronting. Having gone through this process myself, it wasn't easy—it was hard, confronting and often overwhelming. But even in the tough moments, I found tiny slivers of light and, occasionally, something to laugh about. Because, honestly, sometimes if you don't laugh, you'll cry—and I'd done enough of that.

One of those moments came when I decided to reframe my financial situation. I named my new spreadsheet 'My budget without the baggage'. Spoiler alert: The 'baggage' was my ex—or more accurately, his spending habits. It's not that he was a big spender. We just had very different priorities and values, and that's always tricky in a relationship. He saw my love of handbags as completely ridiculous and unnecessary, which, to be fair, I can understand, but I felt exactly the same about some of the things he wanted to spend money on.

And I now no longer had to account for expenses that didn't align with my goals. I didn't have to plan around purchases that didn't light me up. Because honestly, how many surfboards does one person need? (Valid question from a non-surfer... handbags, on the other hand—totally essential.)

Of course, this is just a tongue-in-cheek example, but the shift was powerful. Reframing my budget as something that was *mine* (something that reflected *my* priorities) wasn't just practical, it was *empowering*.

What will you call your new budget? I've seen some great ones, such as the 'Bye-Bye Broke Budget', 'Rise and Thrive' and the 'Broke to Boujee Budget'.

Jot down some ideas here.

_____

_____

_____

_____

_____

Setting yourself up for success

As I've said many times: Systems and habits are what keep your financial plans on track. And when it comes to budgeting, your bank account setup is your support system.

The way you structure your accounts will either set you up for success or make budgeting way harder than it needs to be. If your money is all mixed up in one account, it's easy to lose track of what it's for and where it's going. With the right setup, your budget should run itself. The goal should be to have your cashflow running so well that you forget it's payday.

A perfect example of this was when I was coaching a client who came to me feeling overwhelmed by her day-to-day money management. Every planned expense was categorised and mapped out in a spreadsheet for the next 12 months, with funds automatically allocated fortnightly into separate accounts for annual expenses. On the surface, she was doing everything right: automation, detailed tracking, proactive planning, yet she still felt out of control. Even though everything was accounted for, she was still getting accounts overdrawn and having to move money around, leaving her frustrated and questioning her ability to manage money. She was allowing thoughts of 'I'm just bad at money' to creep in.

When we dug a little deeper, we realised the issue wasn't her effort—or even the budget itself. The real problem was the way her support system (aka her bank account structure) was set up. Her accounts didn't match the way she categorised her expenses in the spreadsheet.

She had a few different accounts that acted as holding zones for various bills, but the mismatch came down to which expenses were being paid from which accounts. Some were fixed, some variable, and some discretionary spending was mixed in too. The problem with that is, if you overspend in one area, it's hard to catch until a big fixed bill hits—and suddenly the money you thought was there... isn't.

So, we didn't throw the whole system out. Instead, we made a few small, intentional tweaks. We regrouped her expenses into clearer buckets like 'fixed bills', 'variable bills', and 'household costs' in a way that actually made sense to her and her life. Then we matched those categories with specific bank accounts and automated what we could.

These changes ensured that her budget and bank accounts worked seamlessly together and became a support system.

The result? A cashflow plan that felt intuitive and manageable, giving her the clarity and confidence she needed. Within four weeks (yes, things take time) everything was adjusted and working like a well-oiled machine.

What works for someone else might not work for you, and what worked for you in the past might not serve you in the future. Sometimes, a small adjustment can transform frustration into empowerment.

Your successful structure

Think of your bank accounts as the framework that holds your financial habits together. The way you set them up can either make life easier or, just like my client found, create unnecessary friction. Structuring your finances effectively isn't just about organising your money. It's about creating a financial ecosystem that supports the habits you need to set you up for success.

I recommend you start with four key bank accounts.

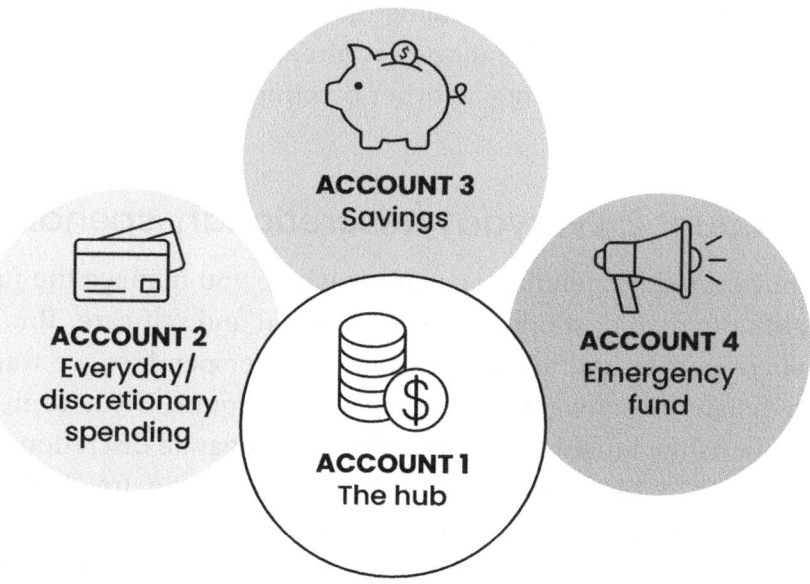

ACCOUNT 3
Savings

ACCOUNT 2
Everyday/
discretionary
spending

ACCOUNT 4
Emergency
fund

ACCOUNT 1
The hub

Account 1: The hub

Think of the hub as the heart of your financial system. It's your main account, the place where all your income flows in and all your expenses flow out. For most people, this also doubles as a bills and expenses account. If you're in a relationship, both partners' incomes or a set amount from those incomes can funnel into this hub, making it easier to track and automate your finances.

The secret to the hub? Automation. Every dollar that lands in this account should be assigned a job, ensuring there's no money sitting idle. Even if you are doing a percentage split budget (more on this in Chapter 11), the money in this account should have a job. Any leftover money isn't 'extra'. It's allocated to upcoming expenses so you're never tempted to dip into it.

Recurring expenses like rent, mortgage payments, insurance and utilities are prime candidates for automation. Start by adding up your annual bills and dividing the total by your pay periods. That money builds up in this account. That way, when a bill arrives, the money is already there: no stress, no scrambling, no stopping all other commitments that week just to pay this bill.

Account 2: Everyday/discretionary spending

Your everyday spending account is where you manage the fun stuff: dining out, shopping, entertainment and self-care. This is where people tend to most commonly overspend, so we want to isolate these 'wants' into their own account. If you're in a relationship, I highly recommend having separate discretionary accounts. Why? Because it gives you both the freedom to spend without guilt or needing to check in. This is your 'no questions asked' money, perfect for those little indulgences that bring you joy.

Account 3: Savings

Segmenting your savings into dedicated 'buckets' is a game changer. Whether you're saving for a holiday, a car, a new home or something else, having separate accounts for each goal makes your progress more transparent. When you can see your funds growing for specific purposes, it's easier to stay motivated.

Automate transfers into these accounts on payday. It takes the temptation out of the equation and ensures your savings are always on track. This simple system turns vague financial aspirations into concrete, achievable goals.

Account 4: Emergency fund

And, of course, there's your emergency fund: your financial safety net and stress-reducer in life's unexpected moments. It's there to catch you when things go sideways, turning potential crises into manageable hiccups. (If you need a refresher on why this fund deserves its own dedicated account, flip back to Chapter 2.)

Can you have too many bank accounts?

Personally, I don't think so (within reason, of course). Having multiple accounts with clearly defined purposes (like your hub, savings and spending accounts) can bring clarity and organisation to your financial life.

You might find it helpful to break things down even further:

- *Fixed bills/expenses account:* This account is for bills and consistent costs, such as rent, mortgage payments and insurance.

- *Variable bills/expenses account:* Some costs fluctuate, such as utilities or subscriptions, and this account should cover those costs.

- *Debt-repayment account:* It makes sense to have a dedicated account for any loan repayments.

- *Food and fuel account:* I like to keep a separate account for groceries and petrol as these are two areas where overspending often happens.

- *Tax account:* If you're self-employed or building assets that might result in a tax bill, set aside money in a separate account to avoid surprises come tax time.

Find a system that works for you, tweak it as needed, and let it empower you to stay in control of your financial journey.

At the end of the day, your bank account structure is there to support your habits, not complicate them.

Reset now: Complete a bank account audit

What accounts do you already have and what do you need?

CURRENT ACCOUNTS	ACCOUNTS I NEED

Action plan

Think of some manageable and actionable steps you can take to shift your current banking and budgeting system to one that is more aligned with your goals and works with your schedule. For example, you may decide to close your online account with Bank No. 1, and open two online dedicated saving accounts with Bank No. 2. Perhaps you will update your direct debits to automate payments from your hub account to an account with Bank No. 3.

Your turn:

_____

_____

_____

_____

_____

Self-employed? This part is for you!

Budgeting is tricky enough, but when your income isn't predictable, it takes an extra level of planning. The good news? With the right setup, you can create a budget that works *with* your fluctuating income, not against it.

If you're struggling with some of the steps we've just covered, then modify your budget process slightly according to this next part.

Find your baseline income

Since your income changes month to month, you need to get a feel for the average flow of money coming in. Look at your last six to 12 months of income and figure out your:

- average monthly income
- lowest earning month (this one is super important!)
- highest earning month.

To keep your budget stable, base your income on your lowest month, not your best one. This stops you from getting caught short when business slows down.

Prioritise fixed expenses first

Now, work out your non-negotiables (the bare minimum you need to cover each month, no matter what). Think: rent/mortgage, bills, groceries, transport and debt repayments.

Once those are covered, you can decide how much goes towards savings, investments and fun stuff when you have a higher-income month.

Build your buffer fund

Since your income isn't consistent, you need a buffer to smooth out the highs and lows.

- When income is high, put extra cash aside to cover low-income months.
- Aim to save at least one to three months' worth of essential expenses in a separate account.
- Think of it as paying yourself a steady wage, even when your earnings fluctuate.

This is where the flow budget comes in. Instead of strict weekly or monthly limits, you work with the natural flow of your income. When cash is coming in strong, top up your buffer and fund your goals. When things are quieter, draw from your buffer instead of scrambling to cut expenses.

Use separate accounts to stay organised

Self-employed finances can get messy fast, so keeping things structured will make life way easier. Some of the different accounts you might consider include a:

- *Business account:* All income lands here first.

- *Tax account:* Automatically set aside a percentage of each payment for tax (so you don't get a nasty surprise at tax time).

- *Buffer account:* Establish your flow fund to cover the slow months.

- *Personal account:* Pay yourself a consistent 'salary' each month based on your budget.

This keeps your business and personal finances separate and makes it easy to see *exactly* what's available to spend, save or reinvest.

Plan for tax and super

Unlike employees, no one is automatically taking tax out of your income — that's on you.

- An accountant or an online calculator can help you work out what your tax might be for the year, but generally, for most, putting aside at least 20 per cent of every payment into a separate tax account is a good rule of thumb.

- If you need to pay GST, set that portion aside immediately so it's ready when BAS (business activity statement) time rolls around.

- Don't forget super: If you're not paying into it, future you is missing out. Even small, regular contributions will add up over time.

Be flexible and check in regularly

Your budget isn't something you set and forget. Every month, check:

- what came in versus what went out

- whether you're building your buffer fund for low-income months

- whether you need to adjust your spending, savings or goals

- if you had extra income, where the best place to put it is.

Being self-employed means income swings are part of the game, but with the right budget and structure, you can create stability — even when your paycheque looks different every month.

Whatever your structure or make up, a budget isn't something to fear. It's a tool.

Instead of cringing at the word 'budget', learn how to make it work for you to give you clarity and control over your cashflow.

Chapter 6

Boosting your income

When life gets tough, what's your first instinct when it comes to money? I'd bet you go straight into survival mode: Tighten the belt, batten down the hatches and figure out where you can cut costs. It's a logical reaction and, as I highlighted earlier, it's a lever you should be considering, but it's not the only one.

So, while cutting unnecessary expenses is important, we also need to acknowledge that there is a limit to how much you can cut. However, there's no limit to how much you can earn.

Let that sink in.

There is a cap on what you can reduce; there's no cap on what you can earn.

That said, earning more isn't a magic wand. If you don't address your habits (overspending, avoidance or a lack of discipline), a bigger paycheque won't solve much. In fact, it could make things worse. Why? Because if you haven't done the work to address the beliefs, patterns and habits we talked about earlier, earning more might feel like pouring water into a leaky bucket.

Hello, lifestyle creep (or lifestyle inflation). It starts small (more dinners out, splurging on small luxuries that used to feel like treats), then it escalates (upgrading your car, moving to a bigger house). None of this is inherently bad. Money is a tool, and you should enjoy it. But if your spending grows in lockstep with your income, you're not building wealth, you're just treading water, or worse, drowning.

The danger with lifestyle creep is that it feels justified. You've worked hard, you've earned it, so why not enjoy it? And you *should* enjoy it — but not at the expense of your long-term goals.

The solution isn't to deprive yourself; it's to find balance. If your lever is to create more income, have a plan for that money from day one. Where is that extra income going and why is that important? How does that move the needle and get you closer to your non-negotiables, and the future you dream of.

When I work with clients on creating more income, they have a clear plan for every extra dollar before it even comes in. The most common priorities? Building an emergency fund, starting a holiday savings account, paying off debt or investing in assets that generate passive income. That's exactly what we're going to do together in the rest of this book.

How to increase your income

When we think of earning, most of us default to employment — trading time for money. This is *active income*. You are doing something for it. The other type is *passive income*. This is the one you hear about when people talk about investing, when your money is doing the hard work and earning you an income.

Focusing on your active income is the starting point for creating financial security. Once you are on your feet and covering expenses, then you can then start to focus on using that active income to create assets that provide a passive income.

There's no one-size-fits-all way to earn more, but if boosting your income is the lever you need to pull, below are some ideas to get you started.

Idea 1: Re-entering the workforce

If you've been out of the paid workforce for a while, stepping back in can feel overwhelming — but it's also an exciting opportunity to reassess your goals and design a career that works for you. Rather than just picking up where you left off, think of this as a chance to realign your work with your lifestyle, values and financial needs.

There are many reasons you might be returning to paid work. Maybe you took time off to raise children, care for a family member or focus on your health, and now a major life change, like a divorce or redundancy, has made you rethink your financial independence. Or maybe you're simply ready for a new challenge and a sense of purpose outside your home life.

Whatever the reason, this is your chance to consider what truly matters to you. Are you looking for part-time flexibility to balance family life? A career pivot that aligns with your passions? A role that provides financial security and growth opportunities? What skills have you gained during your time away that could be valuable in a new role?

Idea 2: Negotiating a pay rise

Asking for a raise is one of the quickest ways to increase your income. After all, if you don't ask, you don't get.

Negotiating a pay rise doesn't have to feel awkward or intimidating. With the right prep, you can confidently approach the conversation and set yourself up for success.

Here's how to make it happen:

- *Do your homework:* Know your worth! Take some time to research what people in similar roles are earning — both inside your company and at others. Websites like Seek can be great for this. You want to walk into that meeting knowing you're asking for something reasonable, not shooting for the moon, or worse — underselling yourself.

- *Keep your receipts:* No one remembers your wins better than you do, so start keeping track. Have you smashed any big projects, taken on extra responsibilities or been given glowing feedback? Write it all down! A solid list of your achievements makes it easier to show how you've added value to the team, and it's easy to forget these things when you are under pressure, so be prepared.

- *Set the scene:* As tempting as it might be to blurt out, 'I want a pay rise' while grabbing a coffee in the communal kitchen, resist the urge. Schedule a proper meeting with your boss and let them know you'd like to discuss your performance and compensation. This gives them time to prepare too, which will make the conversation smoother.

- *Sell yourself:* Frame the conversation around what *you've brought to the table.* Instead of focusing on why you need a pay rise, highlight how you've contributed to the team's success. For example, 'This project I led brought in X results' is far more compelling than 'My rent just went up'.

- *Be open to perks:* If a salary bump isn't on the cards right now, don't let that meeting end without exploring other options. Could you score extra annual leave? More flexibility to work from home? A professional development course you've been eyeing? Perks can add value to your life even if a pay rise isn't on the table.

- *Don't take no as the final answer:* If your boss says now isn't the right time, ask when you can revisit the conversation. Even better, agree on clear targets or goals that could justify a raise in the future. That way, you're not left in limbo wondering what it'll take to get there.

Idea 3: Increasing your prices (if you're self-employed)

Raising your prices can feel daunting, but it's a necessary step in growing a sustainable business. Whether you're a freelancer, consultant or business owner, increasing your rates ensures your work remains profitable and reflects the value you provide.

Start by reviewing your pricing strategy: Are you charging based on industry standards, the transformation you deliver or simply what you've always charged? If you haven't adjusted your prices in a while, inflation, increased expertise and demand for your services might justify a rate increase.

Reframe how you think about pricing: You're not charging for the minutes it takes to do the work, but for the years of experience, skills and problem-solving ability you bring to the table. Clients aren't just paying for a service; they're paying for the confidence, ease and results your expertise delivers.

Idea 4: Exploring side hustles

A side hustle can be a fun and flexible way to turn your skills, assets or hobbies into extra income. The gig economy offers plenty of options, whether you want to freelance, teach, rent out what you own or monetise your creative talents. Here are a few ideas:

- *Freelancing:* Use your skills in writing, admin, design, coding or social media to work with clients remotely. There are platforms that connect freelancers with businesses worldwide, or you can look for direct opportunities. Driving and delivery roles also fall into this category.

- *Teach or tutor:* Offer tutoring in academic subjects, teach skills like music or languages, or create online courses to share your expertise.

- *Rent out your assets:* Turn unused spaces or belongings into income by renting out a spare room, your car or even storage space in your home. Think about what's sitting around that could be making you money.

- *Turn hobbies into income:* Sell handmade goods, monetise photography, or offer services like gardening, craft or home organisation. Pet-sitting or house-sitting can also be a great way to earn extra cash.

- *Casual or seasonal work:* Take on part-time retail jobs, event staffing or short-term roles when demand is high.

- *Surveys and market research:* Earn small amounts through paid surveys, focus groups or product testing.

- *Content creation:* If you enjoy writing, podcasting or making videos, you can generate income through ad revenue, sponsorships or paid subscriptions.

Don't let your brain shortcut your decision and immediately dismiss any of these income-boosting ideas. Before you give all the reasons why it wouldn't work, why it's not an option or why your current path is the only way, pause. With a little creativity, you might just find a side hustle that fits your lifestyle and financial goals.

Remember, you're in a period of great transformation. What worked in the past might not work now, and equally, what didn't work then, might work now.

Reset now: Add income (yay!)

Let's explore each of these income-generating ideas, together.

Think about each idea for adding income in turn, and without judgement, work through the possibilities for you. There are no right or wrong answers here, and we're not even committing yet to doing them!

Which one of the following could you explore?

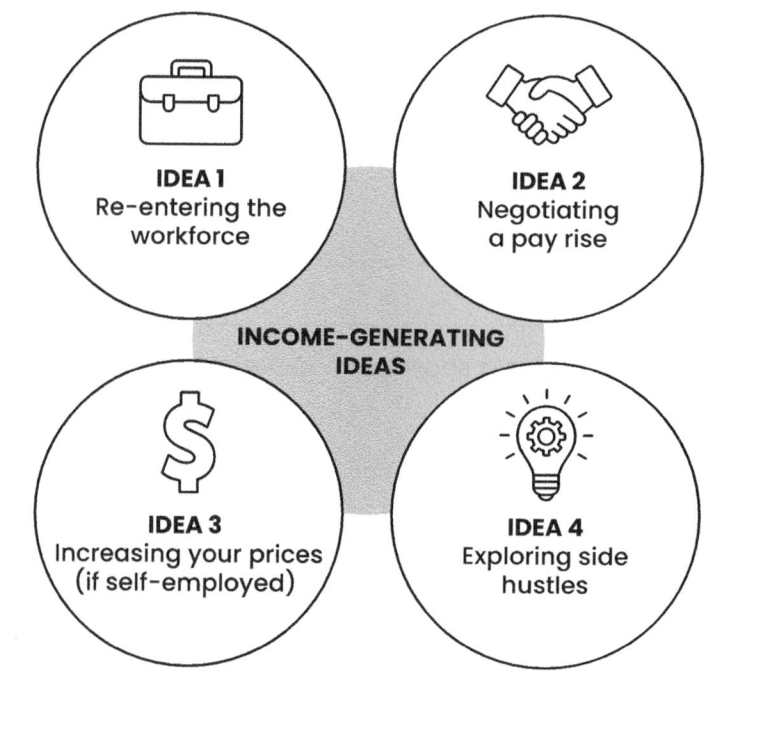

IDEA 1
Re-entering the workforce

IDEA 2
Negotiating a pay rise

INCOME-GENERATING IDEAS

IDEA 3
Increasing your prices (if self-employed)

IDEA 4
Exploring side hustles

(continued)

Step 1: Challenge your first response

For each idea that is relevant to you, ask yourself:

What would it take to make this work for me?

_____

_____

If I had to make this happen, what would be my first step?

_____

_____

What skills, resources or connections do I already have that could help?

_____

_____

What beliefs or assumptions are making me resist this idea?

_____

_____

Could this work as a short-term experiment rather than a permanent change?

_____

_____

What's the best-case scenario if I tried this?

_____

_____

Draw up a table like the one opposite to write down your thoughts. Challenge any responses that are an automatic no, and see if there's a maybe hidden beneath it.

IDEA	PRO	CON	VIABLE YES/NO
Example: Ask for a pay rise	*Extra income in my current job with flexibility for the school run each day*	*Potentially higher expectations and targets*	*Yes*

Step 2: Narrow it down

After giving each option genuine thought, which ones are still on the table? Cross out the ones that truly don't align with, or are not relevant to, your values, lifestyle or skills *after* you've fully considered them. What's left?

Step 3: Apply the sleep-at-night test

For the remaining options, run them through the sleep-at-night test from Chapter 2. Ask yourself the following questions:

- Would pursuing this option cause unnecessary stress or does it feel exciting?
- Can I see myself realistically integrating this into my life?
- Will this improve my financial situation in a way that aligns with my long-term goals?

Step 4: Act now!

Now you have options that feel possible and aligned, pick one or two and outline your first three action steps. What's the very first thing you need to do to move this forward? Set a date to get started.

The goal isn't to have a perfect plan — it's to start moving.

Extra income = extra responsibilities (like tax!)

Earning more is fantastic. It opens up opportunities, gives you freedom and helps you reach your goals faster. Just remember to check if you need insurance for certain activities (such as public liability in the event a customer makes a claim against you), and always be mindful of your capacity. Hustling might be necessary to help you get back on your feet (it can be your slingshot forward), but be cautious of burnout and focus on what feels manageable.

Also, extra income comes with extra responsibilities, and one of the big ones is tax. Whether it's from a pay rise, a second job or a side hustle, more income generally means more tax, so it's important to plan ahead to avoid any surprises come tax time.

It doesn't mean you shouldn't take a second job or a pay rise because you are worried about having to pay more tax.

Australia's tax system is progressive, which means the more you earn, the higher the tax rate on each portion of your income. But here's the important part: You're not taxed at one flat rate across your entire income. Only the income within each tax bracket is taxed at that bracket's rate.

Imagine your income is a plate of cupcakes.

- Your first cupcake (the first $18 200 you earn) is completely tax-free. You get to keep the whole thing — no crumbs taken!

- For your next few cupcakes (income between $18 201 and $45 000), you hand over a small slice: 16 per cent to be exact.

- Then, as your cupcake stack grows (income from $45 001 to $135 000), a slightly bigger slice (30 per cent) goes to tax.

But here's the key: Only the cupcakes in each bracket are taxed at that rate. You're never giving up half your entire stack, just a portion of the ones in the higher brackets.

On top of income tax, if you're in Australia, there's the Medicare levy (2 per cent of your taxable income), which helps fund the public healthcare system. If you're a high-income earner without private health insurance, you might also pay the Medicare levy surcharge, an extra 1 to 1.5 per cent depending on how much you earn.

It might sound complicated, but the system is designed to be fair, with higher earners contributing more while still keeping plenty of their earnings. Once you understand how it works, you'll feel more in control and confident about planning your finances. And if you ever feel overwhelmed, just picture the plate of cupcakes. You'll never look at tax the same way again!

With a little planning and understanding, you can navigate tax with confidence and keep your financial goals on track.

Busting tax myths!

Here are the three most common tax myths I hear.

Myth 1: A pay rise will push me into the next tax bracket

Yes, earning more might push part of your income into a higher tax bracket, but (as we just learned with our plate of cupcakes) *only the portion above that threshold is taxed at the higher rate.* The rest of your income is taxed at the lower rates, so you'll still end up taking home more overall. Don't let this myth hold you back from going for that raise or promotion.

Myth 2: A second job means I'll pay more tax

Taking on a second job doesn't mean you're taxed more overall. What it does mean is that you can only claim the tax-free threshold on one job. For your second job, tax is withheld from the first dollar you earn to make sure you don't underpay during the year.

This withholding can make it feel like you're paying more tax, but when you lodge your tax return, your total income is reconciled. If you've overpaid, the Australian Tax Office (ATO) will refund the difference.

Myth 3: Tax refunds are free money

No! A tax refund isn't a bonus — it's money you overpaid during the year. Think of it as an interest-free loan you gave the ATO. While it's nice to get a lump sum back, wouldn't you rather have that money working for you throughout the year instead?

Reclaim your future self

So we've covered optimising your expenses and increasing income; next let's focus on debt. Because let's face it: It's big expenses that can hold many of us back. Carrying debt can be like dragging extra weight uphill, slowing your climb no matter how much you're earning or cutting from your expenses.

Chapter 7

Doubling down on debt

Like budgeting, debt gets a bad rap. It's misunderstood, oversimplified and feared. Why? Money, in general, can stir up a whole lot of emotions, so money that isn't ours (aka debt) can quickly turn into shame, guilt and overwhelm when we're managing it.

Debt has a reputation for being the enemy — something to escape from, a burden that never loosens its grip. But the truth is, debt is just a tool. It's how you use it that determines whether it helps or hinders you. Avoiding it completely isn't the answer. The key is knowing when to use it, how to handle it and making sure it's working for you — not against you.

I've worked with a lot of people, and in my experience, most people don't reach their financial goals without using some form of debt at some stage in their lives. Many even made mistakes with it, dusted themselves off and went on to use debt again — just smarter the next time.

The goal isn't to fear debt but to use it wisely. A mortgage can help you buy a home. A loan might fund a business that changes your life. Even a credit card (when used right) can be a handy tool (more on that on page 118). Debt can help us create amazing lives, achieve big goals, access things that bring joy and fulfilment and, honestly, even get us out of situations that aren't safe or sustainable. The problem isn't debt itself: it's when it controls you instead of the other way around.

It all comes down to management: understanding the risks, minimising them and making sure debt is a stepping stone, not a stumbling block. When used well, it can be a powerful tool. When mismanaged, it can take you off course just as fast. Let's make sure it's the former.

Debt, like many areas of our financial lives, can get a little muddled, murky and overcomplicated, so the first step with debt is to get it back to basics.

Debt can open doors for wealth when you use it wisely, so we need to get it under control and working for you first.

Understanding different debts

The labels *good debt* and *bad debt* are often used to distinguish between debt that works for you and debt that works against you. While I don't necessarily agree that debt is strictly good or bad, these terms can be helpful when assessing the impact debt has on your financial future.

Good debt is typically tied to investments or assets that increase in value over time or help you generate income. It's often secured, meaning the lender (typically a bank) has collateral (like a house or business asset) it can claim if you fail to repay. This lowers the risk, which is why good debt generally comes with lower interest rates. It can also contribute to building wealth and may offer tax benefits.

Examples include:

- *Mortgages:* Real estate can appreciate over time, building equity and wealth.

- *Student loans:* Education can increase your earning potential, making it an investment in your future.

- *Business loans:* Borrowing to grow a business can create long-term financial returns that outweigh the cost of the loan.

Bad debt is typically linked to purchases that lose value quickly and don't generate income. It's usually unsecured, meaning there's no asset backing the loan. Because lenders take on more risk, bad debt comes with higher interest rates, making it harder to pay off.

Even worse, bad debt can be sneaky. It's often marketed as something helpful or necessary (yes, I'm looking at you, buy-now-pay-later schemes disguised as budgeting tools), but these types of debt can drain your financial resources and make it harder to get ahead.

Common forms of bad debt include:

- *Personal loans:* Borrowing for holidays, shopping sprees or other short-term expenses falls into the bad debt category.

- *Car loans:* Vehicles lose value the moment you drive them out of the car yard, yet many people take out long-term loans to finance them.

- *Buy-now-pay-later services:* These encourage overspending and can lead to mounting balances if not managed carefully.

- *Credit card debt:* High interest rates make it easy to get trapped in a cycle of debt that's hard to escape.

The credit trap

I want to take a moment to talk more about credit cards. Why? Because they're one of the most common financial challenges I see.

Let me be clear: I don't think credit cards are bad. The issue isn't the card itself. It's how people use them that often leads to financial stress.

Yes, credit cards offer convenience and rewards, but let's not forget — banks aren't handing out perks out of the kindness of their hearts. They're in the business of making money, and if you're not careful, the costs can far outweigh the benefits.

A lot of people love credit cards for the bonus points, cashback, travel perks and even insurance. In theory, these sound great. But in reality? I haven't seen too many people actually come out ahead. Yes, some do, but not most. Even if you're disciplined and pay your balance off in full every month, the little fees can sneak up on you: surcharges every time you tap, annual fees and late charges if you slip up even once. Over time, those 'free' rewards you're earning might be costing you more than they're worth.

Credit cards (just like buy-now-pay-later) make it way too easy to spend more than you otherwise would. Studies show that people spend anywhere from 12 to 40 per cent more when using a credit card instead of cash or a debit card. Why? Because when you're not physically handing over money, the pain of spending just isn't the same. It feels less real.

I know, for me, every time I've had a credit card, I've spent more on things I didn't need or even really want. I identified a pattern: When I used a credit card, my spending habits changed. So years ago, I made the call: Credit cards just aren't for me. Do I get a little envious when I see people posting about their free business class upgrade or Bali trip paid for with points? Absolutely. But, for me, the trade-off isn't worth it. Credit cards require a level of discipline that, honestly, I don't have when I use one. So instead of trying to force it, I cut it — literally.

Is it really interest-free?

Another common misconception I hear all the time is about the 'interest-free period'. You see credit cards advertised with 'up to 55 days interest-free', and people assume that means they have 55 days from the date of purchase to pay it back without interest. Not quite. The key words here are 'up to'.

The interest-free period actually starts at the beginning of your statement cycle, not when you make a purchase. If you buy something on the first day of your cycle, yes, you get the full 55 days before interest kicks in. But if you buy something near the end of your statement period? You might only get a couple of weeks or even days before it's due. And if you don't clear your full balance by the due date? You generally won't be eligible for the interest-free period. That means for every dollar you spend from day one you are paying interest. To get an interest-free period on future purchases, you need to ensure you are paying off your due balance in full every single month.

So, while credit cards can be a useful tool for some, they require a lot of discipline to actually work in your favour. If you don't have that discipline, like I don't, you shouldn't have a credit card.

Managing multiple debts — whether it's buy-now-pay-later, credit cards or personal loans — can feel overwhelming, like you're barely keeping your head above water. The good news? There are tried-and-tested strategies to help you take control. And, as with most things in finance, you have options. The key is choosing the approach that works best for you.

But before we dive into the debt you have and any repayment strategies you may need to adopt, let's take a moment to acknowledge where you are, let go of any guilt and refocus on moving forward with a lot less burden.

Acknowledge, forgive and take responsibility

Debt often carries a heavy emotional weight: Feelings of shame, guilt and regret are common. Life happens, and the choices we've made or the circumstances that have led us into financial struggle often feel deeply personal. It's easy to see debt as more than just numbers on a statement, as if it reflects something about our worth or character.

But those feelings of shame won't help you move forward. Instead, they can keep you stuck, repeating patterns and behaviours that reinforce the very cycle you're trying to break. That's why it's so important to practise self-forgiveness when it comes to past financial decisions.

By taking a realistic look at the debt you have now, you can take control of it. It's empowering to know your financial position and have a plan to get you where you would ideally like to be and to achieve the financial life goals you set in Chapter 4. It's also important to recognise your relationship with debt and money and identify when you are slipping back into old habits.

What's going on around us, combined with the deep-rooted beliefs we've formed from a young age, can subtly but powerfully shape our financial behaviours. This often manifests as overspending to cope with emotions, avoiding bank statements out of fear or repeating habits that provide short-term relief but cause long-term harm.

Recognising and forgiving your choices is the first step to breaking free.

Reset now: Recognising your habits

Take an honest, non-judgemental look at the circumstances, habits or decisions that contributed to your current financial situation.

Have a look at the debts you tallied (if any!) in your net worth exercise in Chapter 1.

Complete the following steps.

Step 1: Acknowledge what got you here

Ask yourself the following questions.

- How did these debts come about and why?

- How do you feel about these debts?

- Were there moments when you felt like you had no other option than to get into debt?

- Did any of these debts result from overspending, unexpected life events or financial habits?

- Would you make the same choices given the opportunity today?

- The goal here isn't to assign blame. It's to identify patterns so you can move forward with clarity and avoid repeating the same cycle.

(continued)

Step 2: Practise forgiveness

Now, let's release the guilt. Read this statement aloud (or write it down if that feels more powerful): *I did the best I could with the knowledge, resources and circumstances I had at the time. Now, I choose to move forward with greater awareness and control.*

Then, reflect on these questions:

- What lessons have you learned from your past financial decisions?

- How can these lessons help you make better choices moving forward?

- If you were giving advice to a friend in your situation, what would you tell them?

Forgiveness isn't about excusing past mistakes. It's about freeing yourself from shame so you can take action from a place of empowerment, not guilt.

Step 3: Take responsibility

Shift your focus to what's *possible* moving forward. You may not have all the answers yet, and that's okay. The goal right now isn't to solve everything at once, but to commit to change and take that first step.

- What's one small step you can take today to *feel more in control* of your financial situation (e.g., checking your balances, listing your debts, setting a reminder to review your spending habits)?

- What's one *commitment* you can make to yourself about how you want to approach your finances moving forward (e.g., to be more intentional with money or no longer ignoring your financial situation)?

- What's one *empowering statement* you can repeat when financial stress creeps in? (e.g., 'I have the power to change my financial future' or 'This is a challenge I can overcome')?

Set your intention to move forward with clarity and confidence.

Repayment strategies

Having a plan to tackle debt is like setting a goal with a clear direction: It keeps you focused, motivated and in control. Without a strategy, it's easy to feel stuck or overwhelmed, making it harder to make real progress.

For me, I know that having a plan (no matter how slow and steady the progress might be) helps me feel in control.

Most of my clients feel the same way. When you're juggling multiple debts and just covering minimum repayments, it can feel like you're not really getting anywhere. That frustration can be exhausting. But having a clear plan changes everything. Instead of feeling powerless, you suddenly have a real path forward and can see the light at the end of the tunnel.

There are three main debt management methods to choose from, and yes, each one can work. The key is finding the approach that feels right for you. Choose one that is going to make you feel like you're making progress and that feels the most sustainable. So, let's go through each one.

Option 1: The avalanche method

This method prioritises paying off debts with the highest interest rates first while making minimum payments on the rest. It's the most financially efficient strategy because it reduces the total amount of interest paid over time.

Why I love this one: Math-wise, it works. It saves you the most money in the long run. By knocking out high-interest debts first, you pay less overall and get out of debt faster.

Why I don't love this one: It can feel slow. If your highest-interest debt is also your biggest balance, it might take a while to see real progress, which can be demotivating. You need patience and discipline to stick with it.

How to do it:

- List all your debts in order from the highest to lowest interest rate.

- Focus on putting extra money towards the highest-interest debt while making minimum payments on the rest.

- Once the highest-interest debt is paid off, roll that payment into the next highest, and keep going.

Option 2: The snowball method

This method focuses on paying off the smallest debt first, regardless of interest rate. Once that debt is cleared, you roll that payment into the next smallest debt, and so on.

Why I love this one: It builds momentum. I'm the kind of person who loves a list. If I do something that wasn't on my list, 1: I'm a little annoyed, and 2: I'll add it just to cross it off. So, this approach works perfectly for brains like mine. Knocking out a debt (no matter how small) feels like a win. And if you've got a bunch of little ones, you'll be ticking them off fast, which keeps you motivated to keep going.

Why I don't love this one: It's not the most cost-effective. Since you're ignoring interest rates, you might end up paying more in the long run compared with the avalanche method.

How to do it:

- List all your debts in order from the smallest to largest balance.

- Focus on paying off the smallest debt first while making minimum payments on the rest.

- Once the smallest debt is paid off, roll that payment into the next smallest, and repeat.

Option 3: Debt consolidation

This strategy combines multiple debts into one loan, ideally with a lower interest rate, making repayments easier to manage. It's similar to a credit card balance transfer, where you move high-interest debt onto a lower-rate option.

Why I love this one: Its simple! Everything wrapped up into one payment — what's not to love?

Why I don't love this one: It's not the quick fix people think it is. In my experience, it can lead to bigger problems down the track.

How to do it:

- Speak with your bank or lender.

- Ensure all other loans and debts are paid out as part of the process.

- Confirm those accounts are closed and repayments have been stopped.

- Be cautious: There are a few things to watch out for.
  - Longer loan terms can cost more overall. For example, rolling a car loan or personal loan into your mortgage might lower your interest rate (e.g., from 12 to 6 per cent), but now that debt is stretched over 30 years instead of three to five years. You might end up paying more in the long run.
  - It doesn't address the root cause. If overspending or lifestyle creep got you into debt, consolidation

won't fix that. It's like mopping up water without fixing the leak: The cycle will continue unless your behaviours change.

Reset now: Break down debt

Now, order your debts based on how you'd like to tackle them:

- highest interest rate first (avalanche method)

- smallest balance first (snowball method)

- combining small debts into one (debt consolidation).

Think about which method is the simplest for you and which makes more sense first. Using the table here, list your debts in the order depending on which repayment method you plan to use.

MY DEBT REPAYMENT PLAN					
Debt name	Minimum repayment	Due date	Interest rate	Pay today	New balance

Remember: You must pay the *minimum amount* for all your debts, no matter which strategy you go with.

Managing your home loan

We've talked a lot about tackling high-interest and consumer debt, but managing property debt (whether it's your home or an investment property) follows a different set of rules. While some of the strategies to pay it down faster might feel familiar, there are unique benefits, risks and approaches when it comes to mortgage management.

It's not just about making repayments on time — it's about structuring your loan so your money is working smarter, not just harder.

Conduct an annual rate review

Regularly reviewing your interest rate can save you thousands over the life of your loan. The less interest you pay, the quicker you'll be able to repay your loan. As a general rule of thumb, I think you need to be reviewing your loan at least once a year. Like with your other debts, negotiating your rate with your lender is important.

Don't be afraid to call your lender and ask for a lower interest rate. Many banks and credit providers are willing to work with you — it's in their interest to keep you on track. The worst they can say is no.

A simple ask is sufficient, such as: 'I'm reviewing my loan and exploring other options. I'd like to discuss a lower interest rate. What is the best rate you can offer?'

For example, on a $500 000 loan over 30 years, reducing the interest rate from 6.5 per cent to 6.2 per cent could save you around $98 per month. Over the life of the loan, that's more than $35 000 in interest saved just from a small rate change.

There are also great negotiation scripts available online, depending on your situation.

Make payments more frequently

One of the simplest strategies is changing how often you make repayments. Moving from monthly to fortnightly or weekly payments can make a big difference. Since there are 26 fortnights in a year, you end up making the equivalent of one extra month's repayment annually without even noticing. Over time, this helps cut down interest and shortens your loan term.

For example, on a $500 000 loan at 6.5 per cent over 30 years, your monthly repayment would be around $3160. If, instead, you pay $1580 every fortnight (half the monthly amount), you'll end up making the equivalent of one extra monthly repayment each year. This small tweak could cut nearly six years off your loan and save you over $145 000 in interest.

Consider making extra repayments

Making extra repayments when you can has a big impact — whether it's a lump sum from a tax refund or just rounding up your regular repayment. Let's say your repayment is $1658, could you round it up to $1700 or even $1750? Even small extra amounts add up over time, reducing the interest you pay and paying off your loan faster.

Extra payments typically go straight off your loan balance, reducing what you owe. Depending on your loan type, these extra payments may sit in 'redraw' and remain accessible for you to get to if you need. But here's the catch: If your goal is to get ahead by getting your loan down, you need the discipline to leave that money there. Constantly redrawing those extra repayments you made defeats the purpose of making extra repayments

The key is sustainability. Don't set yourself up for failure by making extra repayments that aren't realistic, only to dip back into them later. Money is a tool, and the goal is to build strong, sustainable habits.

Offset account versus redraw account

Both offset and redraw accounts help reduce the interest you pay on your home loan, but they work in different ways. Understanding the differences can help you choose the option that best suits your financial situation. Your redraw comes from any extra money you pay off your loan above the minimum repayments. That extra then sits on your loan, reducing the loan balance, so you owe less.

An offset account is a separate bank account that looks and feels just like a normal transaction account, but instead of earning interest, the balance offsets your loan amount.

For example, if you have a $500 000 home loan and $50 000 in your offset account, you'll only be charged interest on $450 000. The key thing to remember is that this doesn't change your repayment amount — you're still making the same repayments, but because less interest is being charged, more of your money goes towards reducing the actual loan balance. This means you'll pay off your loan faster without even changing your repayment schedule.

Why you'd use an offset account

- You want daily access to your money, like a regular transaction account.

- You prefer flexibility and the ability to move money in and out easily.

- You want to keep savings separate from your loan but still reduce interest.

- You're disciplined with money and can manage having easy access without spending it.

- You might turn the property into an investment later and want to preserve tax deductibility.

- You want to use it like a high-powered savings account that helps pay down your loan faster.

- Your lender offers 100 per cent offset (some only offer partial offset).

Why you'd use a redraw facility

- You're happy to 'set and forget' and make extra repayments without needing frequent access.

- You want to reduce the temptation to dip into your savings.

- You prefer a more structured, less flexible way to pay down your loan faster.

- You don't plan to use the property as an investment in future, so tax deductibility isn't a concern.

- Your lender doesn't charge fees or restrictions on accessing the redraw.

- You want to automate extra payments and watch your loan balance reduce over time.

Reset now: Consider your loan options

How would an offset account benefit you?

_____

_____

How would a redraw facility benefit you?

_____

_____

What's one simple action you can take today to optimise your loan?

_____

_____

Specific strategies for life upheavals

Some life plot twists come with unique financial challenges that need extra thought. To help you _refocus_ on what matters most right now, here are some practical tips tailored to different situations so you can keep moving forward, no matter what life throws your way.

Separation

If your name is on it, you're responsible — full stop.

Joint debts with an ex-partner can quickly become a financial nightmare. Even if your ex has the asset (like a house, car or credit card), if your name is still on the loan, you're legally on the hook. Missed payments or financial disputes can directly impact your credit and financial future.

What you can do:

- Monitor joint debts closely to ensure payments are made.

- Work with a legal or financial professional to protect your interests. This could include refinancing debts into your ex's name or ensuring liabilities are addressed in a property settlement.

- Get everything in writing to avoid future misunderstandings.

Job loss

Losing a job is a tough plot twist, but you can stay in control of your debts with the right plan. Without a steady income, the key is acting quickly and prioritising what matters most.

What you can do:

- Review your debts: List balances, due dates and interest rates to get clear on what you owe. The exercise on page 126 can help with this.

- Call your lenders ASAP: Many lenders offer hardship programs that allow you to reduce or pause payments.

- Cut back to essentials: Create a bare-bones budget, prioritising housing, food and utilities. Chapter 5 has all the tools you need to get started with your budget.

- Avoid high-interest debt like credit cards or personal loans unless absolutely necessary. Instead, explore emergency savings, government assistance or community programs such as financial counselling.

Remember: This is temporary. The goal is to stabilise your finances while you work on regaining income.

Death of a spouse

Losing a spouse is devastating, both emotionally and financially. If you shared debts, it's important to get clarity on what happens next.

If you have joint debts, you're typically responsible for continuing the repayments. If the debt is in your spouse's name, these may be handled through their estate, depending on local laws and their available assets.

What you can do:

- Gather financial documents to get a clear picture of all debts and obligations.

- Notify banks/lenders of your spouse's passing to update accounts and discuss repayment options.

- Seek professional advice to understand your legal and financial rights.

- Use life insurance or benefits strategically making sure you balance immediate debt repayment with long-term financial stability (again, professional advice can help you with this).

No matter what kind of financial plot twist you're facing, the key is refocusing, planning and taking control — one step at a time.

What matters is what's next

Debt is just a tool — one that can work for you or against you, depending on how you manage it. You're allowed to make mistakes. But those mistakes don't define your future wealth or your worth. What matters is what you do next.

Chapter 8

Planning your property path

It's not uncommon for a major life shift to send ripples through every aspect of our lives, including where we live. There's something incredibly unsettling about facing a major life change and realising that what should be your safe space might need to change too. It's one of the biggest emotional and financial decisions you'll make, and it often comes at a time when you already feel completely drained.

Whether out of necessity or choice, these changes often force us to reassess our housing situation. The process can be a logistical headache, but it's also deeply emotional and financially complex.

Whichever situation you find yourself in, the most important consideration should be, first, safety and, second, financial feasibility. These two factors must be at the forefront of your decision-making process.

For many, a home is more than just bricks and mortar — it's a symbol of stability, success and security. It might have been your first step of independence, maybe it was the family home where your kids have grown up, or the house you built from scratch or painstakingly renovated with every free minute (like mine).

I've come to learn that home, *to me,* isn't just a physical space. It's a feeling I create, and I can create that anywhere. But that reframing didn't happen overnight. The key is to focus on what truly matters to you and why. And it's okay if, right now, that is different to what it might look like down the track.

My transition from homeowner to renter has been a process — one that brought relief in some ways (goodbye unfinished DIY projects) and a fresh start, but also moments of self-doubt and feelings of failure. Why? Because, like so many financial decisions, home ownership is often tied to our sense of security. And security (especially when it comes to money) is intertwined with our self-worth.

Get it right for you

Property can have a major impact in our lives in two key areas: where you live (your home) and how you build wealth. Sometimes, property ticks both boxes. Other times, it doesn't.

- Do you need somewhere safe and secure to live? *Yes.*
- Does that need to be a home you own? *No.*
- Do you need property to build wealth? *No.*
- Can it help? *Absolutely.*
- Can it hinder? *Without a doubt.*

Of course, there's crossover between investing and property ownership, and sometimes they go hand in hand, but we're not diving deep into investment strategies here. This is about resetting the basics. Once you've got that foundation in place, then you can start dreaming big about how property and future you might be a perfect match.

If there's one lesson to take from this chapter, it's this: Your home should serve you, not the other way around.

Aussies love property — it's quite possibly in our DNA. It's always been a huge part of how we build wealth, and while that mindset is starting to shift, it's still deeply ingrained.

There's something about real estate that feels *real* — a home you can touch, live in and build a life around. Most of us grew up watching our parents or family members buy homes to live in and using property as their main financial lever, reinforcing the idea that owning a home is the ultimate sign of financial security. It's familiar, it's tangible and, for many, it just *feels* safe.

But this isn't the case everywhere. In Germany, renting is the norm, and long-term tenants have rights that give them stability without needing to own. In Japan, property often depreciates rather than appreciates, so people approach real estate very differently. And in the US, while property is part of the wealth-building conversation, the sheer variety of markets means there's no single approach that dominates the way it does in Australia.

The decision to buy or rent isn't just about finances. It's about lifestyle, flexibility and long-term goals — and it's not always a straight choice between one or the other.

Own, rent or both?

Owning a home gives you stability, control and the potential for capital growth. It means you can put down roots, renovate as you like and build equity over time. But it also comes with financial responsibilities: mortgages, rates, maintenance and the reality that property values don't always go up.

Renting, on the other hand, offers flexibility. You're not tied down to a mortgage, you don't have to worry about repairs or upkeep, and you can live in locations that might be unaffordable to buy into. But there's a trade-off: you're subject to rent increases, landlords selling and you won't build equity (well, in that particular property anyway).

I recently spoke with Jill. She's 56, recently separated and renting in Sydney, where she's lived her whole life. Her 25-year-old daughter is still at home, finishing uni. Jill wanted to buy a place for the security of home ownership, but buying in Sydney meant taking on a massive mortgage — one that still wouldn't get her the kind of home or location she actually wanted. And with retirement hopefully only five, maybe ten, years away, that kind of debt felt really risky to Jill. It definitely didn't pass her sleep-at-night test. She also wasn't ready to move just yet — her daughter was in such an important stage in her studies, and Jill didn't want to affect that.

Jill felt completely overwhelmed. She felt like she needed to buy now or it would be too late, given her age and looming goal of retirement.

So, we put the immediate decision aside and looked to the future instead. I asked her to picture *future Jill* ten years from now, retired, her daughter thriving in her career, maybe even travelling the world or settled into her own family home. When she really thought about it, Jill knew she didn't actually want to stay in Sydney long-term. She imagined her retirement in a quiet, beachside town well out of the city.

So why was she stuck thinking she had to either buy now in Sydney or miss out on being a homeowner altogether? Like most things, there are options — it's just hard for us to see them when we are only used to seeing things done one way.

Rent-vesting: The best of both worlds?

Rent-vesting is a strategy where you rent a home that suits your lifestyle while owning property as an investment elsewhere. It's always been a strategy, but it's got itself a bit of a buzzword title now.

Rent-vesting is a way to get onto the property ladder without compromising on where you want to live. Instead of buying in an area that might not align with your lifestyle or budget, you invest in a property that makes financial sense, while still enjoying the flexibility of renting in a location that works for you.

For Jill, this type of approach could work. She could consider buying a property where she wants to be in the future — rent it out for now until she is ready to move there — while renting in Sydney where it makes sense for her and her daughter right now.

Rent-vesting is what I'm currently doing. I owned my home for years, but after my separation, I had to reassess what actually made sense for me. Renting a place that works for my lifestyle while investing elsewhere is right for me at this point in time. Property is still a big part of my wealth-building strategy, and those investments are growing — they'll eventually help me buy a family home if/when the time is right. For now, this setup gives me the freedom to keep moving forward without feeling stuck.

I don't want to sit on the sidelines, waiting until I have the perfect vision of what my future home or life will look like. Instead, I'm making financial moves that keep my options open. Rent-vesting lets me live where I want now while still growing my wealth for the future — maybe it could work for you too?

Of course, there are cost considerations. In a perfect scenario, rent-vesting can put you in a stronger position from a tax and cashflow perspective, but it doesn't always work out that way. And let's be real: The numbers aren't always the most important part. Practical and emotional factors matter just as much.

The goal isn't always to take the most financially optimal path — it's to make choices that add value to your life. If a decision makes sense for you, is financially feasible and doesn't stop you from doing other things that matter, like ensuring your and your future self's financial security, then why not?

It's your life, your money, and as long as you're making an informed choice, that's what really counts.

Navigating your options

The clients I help often have similar situations to me, in that they're newly separated, but their housing options differ. I also help countless clients with other situations that require recalibration that aren't separations.

Depending on your situation, you usually have several options at any one time, even though it often doesn't feel that way. Each option comes with its own financial and emotional implications, so it's essential to think through your long-term goals and financial capacity. Below are some common paths people take.

If you've separated and owned a home together:

- *You keep the home:* This might involve refinancing the mortgage in your name and/or buying out the other party's share.

- *They keep the home:* The other party takes over sole responsibility for the mortgage and/or buys out your share.

- *You sell the property:* Selling may allow you to pay off the mortgage and split the remaining proceeds, which can then be used to start fresh or invest elsewhere.

If you have suffered the loss of your spouse and owned a home together:

- *Stay in the home:* You may decide to remain in the property if it's financially manageable and aligns with your goals.

- *Downsize:* Selling and moving to a smaller, more affordable property can reduce financial pressure and provide flexibility for your new circumstances.

- *Rent it out:* If moving feels right but you're not ready to sell, renting the property could generate income while you decide your next steps.

If you've lost your job or had a significant income reduction and have a home:

- *Downsize:* Selling and moving to a property with lower costs can free up equity and reduce ongoing financial commitments.

- *Sell the property and rent:* Renting may offer flexibility and reduce financial strain during a period of instability.

- *Access assistance:* Explore options like mortgage repayment holidays or refinancing to reduce monthly payments, or seek government support during the transition.

These are just starting points. How your property decisions play out will depend on your unique circumstances. Having a clear understanding of your options and seeking advice to navigate them is crucial to making choices that align with you. And like most things, that goes far deeper than just dollars.

Deciding what to do with your home is not just a financial decision; it's deeply personal and can significantly impact your journey forward.

Testing the waters

If you own your home but staying put doesn't feel quite right and you're not ready to sell, then renting it out while you live elsewhere could give you space to breathe and decide.

Yes, moving can be a hassle (trust me, I know), but it doesn't have to be forever. And if your move, like mine, followed a separation, there's something to be said for avoiding those awkward supermarket run-ins with your ex by moving a suburb or two over.

Renting out your home can buy you time and flexibility, but it's not without its challenges.

Not every property makes a good investment. You'll need to weigh up the rent you could earn against the costs you'll still be covering — things like your mortgage, council rates, insurance, and any expected ongoing maintenance — all while you are paying rent and utilities elsewhere.

- Could you afford it if the rent doesn't cover everything?
- Is there a lot of annoying little maintenance issues that you were happy to let slide but paying tenants wouldn't?

Then think about the bigger picture. Is this a short-term solution while you figure things out, or could this home become a longer-term investment? There may be tax implications too — both while it's being rented and when it's sold later. So once you've had a think, reach out to your accountant or a financial adviser. They can help you see the full picture.

Of course, this kind of strategy isn't for everyone. But I'm simply here to open your mind to what's possible, so you don't feel stuck. You've got options. And there are some helpful tax rules and exemptions that might work in your favour, so call in the experts from your village to help you make the call.

Before you decide, just keep in mind — renting out your home involves more than the financial side. It also comes with a few personal responsibilities, so take a moment to check in with yourself:

- How do you feel about strangers living in your home?
- Do you want to be a landlord?
- Will this choice give you peace of mind or add more stress?

If it passes your sleep-at-night test, it might just be the breathing space you need.

You don't need to go all in straight away

I distinctly recall some lovely clients a few years ago who had just retired and decided to leave their family farm of 40-plus years for a simpler, low-maintenance lifestyle in a luxury oceanfront unit. This was a decision for the lifestyle, not out of financial necessity. They were excited, but as it got closer, they became more and more apprehensive. After all, they had never lived near the ocean and had never lived in an apartment — they hadn't even had close neighbours for decades. After going through their options they decided that, instead of diving straight into selling the farm and buying the apartment, they would rent one first.

What they discovered surprised them — they missed the farm lifestyle and absolutely hated living in an apartment, no matter how great the view was. Within 12 months, they returned to their property, this time adapting the farm and simplifying it to better suit their changing needs. They now plan to continue to enjoy it for as long as possible — an option that wouldn't have been possible if they had sold the property to go all in on what they thought they wanted.

This 'try before you buy' concept is important, and it applies to so many areas of life. It can save you from making expensive mistakes.

I see the same thing happen with retirees dreaming of the grey nomad life — selling up, buying a brand-new caravan and hitting the road. My advice? Coming from someone who's owned a caravan before: *Hire one first*. Actually, hire a few different styles. Test them out, see what works for you and, most importantly, make sure you *like* caravanning before you go all in.

Trying before you buy lets you make smarter, more informed choices — whether it's clothes, a caravan or even bigger life decisions like a home.

Practical versus emotional decisions

We love options — but with options come decisions, and sometimes the hardest part is knowing where to start. If you're unsure whether to stay, sell or rent out your home, here are a few key considerations to help you work through the decision-making process.

- Practical considerations

  - *Safety and security:* Is your current home a safe and suitable environment?

  - *Financial commitments:* Can you afford the mortgage, rent or upkeep in your current financial situation?

  - *Loan eligibility:* If you're taking over a mortgage or considering buying a new property, do you qualify for the lending you need? If you sell a home, will you be able to get a loan in the future when/if the time is right?

  - *Income changes:* If you've experienced a reduction in income, how does that affect your ability to maintain your current housing?

- Emotional considerations:

  - *Attachment and comfort:* Does your current home still feel like the right place for you, or is it filled with memories you're ready to move on from?

  - *Stability:* Does staying provide a sense of stability and security, or do you feel stuck?

  - *Alignment with future goals:* Does keeping the home align with the life you envision for yourself moving forward, whether that's a simpler, more flexible arrangement or a long-term investment?

Each option comes with its own costs: staying put means covering mortgage repayments, rates, insurance and maintenance, while selling brings expenses like agent fees, legal costs and moving costs.

Your goals, values and *why* matter here. A solid budget with different scenarios can help you see the financial impact, but numbers aren't everything.

When you're weighing up your options, check in with yourself and ask the three sleep-at-night questions from Chapter 2. They'll help you cut through the noise and figure out what really feels right.

If you're grieving or navigating a major life transition, it's important to acknowledge that any change can carry an emotional weight and make it much harder to see things clearly.

Reset now: Assess your living options

Take a moment to step back and reflect on your choices and decisions through this exercise.

Where are you living now?

Is it meeting your practical needs?

Is it safe, affordable and sustainable for your current situation?

What are some of your practical considerations?

What are the costs (mortgage, rent, rates, maintenance, moving expenses)?

Does this option make financial sense based on your income and goals?

Is it realistic for the long term?

What are some of your emotional considerations?

How do you feel about staying? Is it the right environment for you?

Is it providing comfort and stability, or do you feel stuck?

Are you holding onto it for the right reasons?

What are all your current options?

List every possibility: staying, selling, renting, downsizing, rent-vesting, moving elsewhere.

_____

_____

_____

_____

_____

Which of these options passes your sleep-at-night test?

Which option gives you the most peace of mind?

If you imagine making the change, does it feel like relief or anxiety?

Does your decision align with the life you want to build?

Taking a step forward

Once you've weighed up the financial and emotional factors, and landed on some options that might work for you, you'll need to put some steps into action.

If *buying* is on the horizon, it's never too early to start preparing:

- Talk to a mortgage broker to understand your borrowing capacity, repayment commitments and whether you qualify for any grants or concessions.

- Get clear on your game plan. Is this a stepping-stone home or a long-term one? Will you eventually rent it out? What's the bigger picture?

- Run the numbers. A mortgage isn't the only cost: factor in rates, maintenance and the less obvious expenses such as gardening, utilities and ongoing upkeep. Will these costs impact other financial goals?

If *renting* or staying put makes more sense for now, that doesn't mean you're standing still. You can still work towards financial security by:

- building your savings or investment strategy so you have flexibility down the track

- making sure your current setup aligns with your long-term goals, whether that's maintaining lifestyle freedom, reducing financial stress or keeping options open.

But note, this step could take some time. Big decisions should not be taken lightly, so please do your due diligence and talk to members of your village.

The key is making the best choice for where you are now, with a plan for what comes next.

Chapter 9
Maximising your super, simply

Before you start snoozing at the very sound of the word *superannuation*, hear me out!

While calling superannuation *sexy* might be a stretch, for many, it is likely to be one of the biggest financial assets you'll ever have, so it deserves your attention. Attention *now*, not when you get older!

Depending on where you are in the world, your retirement savings system might have a different name — whether it's a 401(k) in the US, KiwiSaver in New Zealand or a UK pension scheme. In this chapter, we'll specifically refer to the Australian retirement system called superannuation. Regardless of what it's called, the question is the same: Are you making the most of it?

Super is a massive topic, and like other systems around the world, it's a rabbit hole of rules, strategies and investment options. So if you try to take it all in at once, it can feel overwhelming.

For many people recovering from a major life upheaval, super is either:

- low on their radar because they don't understand it, or
- high on their radar because something has gone wrong, and it's causing stress.

In my experience, major life events (separation, job loss, the death of a loved one) often have a ripple effect on super. Maybe it was split in a divorce settlement, perhaps you had to dip into it during a tough time or you simply stopped making contributions while you were focused on getting through life. It's rare for a financial plot twist to leave your retirement savings unimpacted.

So, my goal here is to make super really simple. Today, we're focusing on why your super is important and steps you can take right now.

That's it. We're not diving into every detail or exploring every possible strategy, because the goal is to get you reset and refocused on what matters. Once you're in a position to focus on building wealth and if you decide that super is a tool you want to maximise, there's plenty of cool stuff to learn. But for now, it's about getting the basics sorted.

A little effort now can make a massive difference in the long run.

What super is (and isn't)

I've been in the financial industry for a long time, and superannuation is ever changing—so much so, it's hard for even the professionals to keep up. Plus, there are a lot of misconceptions. So if you're feeling out of your depth with super. I get it; that's completely valid.

If I had a dollar for every time someone told me they don't trust super, think it's too risky or know someone who 'lost all their money in super', I'd have a lot more dollars in my own super!

So, let's clear up a few things:

- *First, super is your money.* It's not some mystery pot controlled by the government or a faceless institution. It belongs to you. But because it sits in the background (quietly building over the years), it's easy to ignore until it suddenly feels urgent.

- *Second, super itself isn't risky.* Yes, how you choose to invest within super can be risky. But superannuation itself is not an investment — it's a tax structure. Think of it as a vehicle, a tax-advantaged space where your investments are held. Whether your super grows or struggles depends on how you invest the money within it. Shares, property, cash — you have options, and most importantly, you have control.

Whether retirement feels like light years away or just around the corner — there's a lot to love about super. It's one of the most powerful (and underrated) tools for building wealth over time, thanks to its tax benefits and the magic of compounding.

Your superannuation is preserved until you meet certain conditions for its release. For most of us, that's your preservation age, which is 60. You can access it earlier in specific circumstances, such as:

- experiencing severe financial hardship
- facing permanent disability or terminal illness.

If early retirement is your goal, don't write off super just yet — it still plays a big role in your financial future even if you can't touch it until you're older. And if you're planning to live well past 60 (which you should be, because most of us will), super should be a key part of your overall strategy.

The trick is having a plan to bridge the gap until your super becomes accessible. By balancing super with other assets (savings, shares or property), you'll have the flexibility to retire on your terms, whether that's at 55, 65 or beyond.

But your super is *not* just for, or about, retirement.

The one thing I wish more people understood is that super is a powerful financial resource that can offer benefits long before you hit your preservation age.

Super can be *super* handy well before retirement for a few reasons:

Increasing savings

Because super is preserved until retirement, it creates a disciplined savings machine. No dipping into it for impulse buys — it's there to protect your future. Preservation is one of the reasons people don't like it, but I think this is a good thing!

Managing risk

Super funds typically spread your money across various asset classes, which are managed for you, reducing risk and offering more stable returns over time. If the decision was left to individuals, we'd likely see a lot more 'retirement savings' in an investment property that isn't diversified — that's putting all your retirement eggs in one basket, on one street, in one suburb. Eek!

Reducing your tax

Super offers concessional tax rates — both on what you contribute (through work or voluntarily) and on the investment earnings within your fund. That means more of your hard-earned money stays working for you, helping to grow your long-term savings.

Once you have retired after 60, you can generally draw a tax-free income from your super — and the investment returns within your retirement account are usually also tax-free. There are caps and a few considerations to be aware of, but this is definitely one of the standout benefits of using superannuation.

Funding essential insurance

Using your super to pay for insurance premiums can help you maintain crucial coverage without impacting your day-to-day cashflow. This means when cashflow is tight, important insurance like life, total and permanent disability or even income protection insurance doesn't need to be the first to go, it can be funded from your super.

Saving for your first home

Super isn't just for when you're 'old'. It can help you save for your first home and get important insurance without impacting your cashflow. The First Home Super Saver Scheme (FHSSS) allows you to save for a deposit within your super fund, benefiting from the concessional tax treatment. This can accelerate your savings and make homeownership more attainable.

Accessing funds in financial hardship

In times of severe financial hardship, such as unemployment, illness or other emergencies (we saw a lot of this during COVID), you may be able to access your super early. However, this should be a last resort, as it can significantly impact your retirement savings. Always seek financial advice before making early withdrawals.

What steps to take to manage your super

It's easy for me to get carried away with superannuation because I love it. It's been such a major part of my career advising retirees, and I know how important it is as the backbone of a solid financial plan. But I'll refrain from getting too deep in the weeds. Right now we are focusing on just the key things.

Essentially the takeaways are that it's *your money*, you need to know what's happening with it, and small tweaks now could mean tens or even hundreds of thousands *more* in retirement.

So let's get back to some basics and make sure you're set up correctly with your super.

Find your super

When we did your net worth task in Chapter 1, you should have noted your super balance and where it's held. If that slipped your mind at the time, now is the time to check and add it to your net worth tracker.

Locate lost super

If you've worked multiple jobs or moved frequently, you may have lost track of some super accounts. The ATO has an online service through my.gov.au to help you locate lost or unclaimed super. If you find multiple super accounts, you'll likely see an option to 'consolidate' them. *Do not do this just yet.* We'll come back to this on page 171.

Update your details

Get in contact with your fund (or funds) and make sure your personal details are up to date: name, address and date of birth. (You'd be surprised how often date-of-birth errors cause issues later!) Get your login details and set up the app for easy access. Log in to check sections such as 'your details', 'your investments', 'your insurance' and 'your contributions'. If you can't find what you need, call your fund. You're paying admin fees, so don't be afraid to ask for help when you need it.

Clarify investments

A common misconception is that your money is invested within the super fund company. In reality, your super fund invests on your behalf—it is simply the administrator, providing access to a range of investments. Your actual investments (whether shares, property or fixed income) are spread across a variety of companies and assets. If you've never actively chosen an investment option, your super is likely in a default setting based on your age. That's not necessarily a bad thing, but it's important to know what your options are and make informed decisions on what is right for you.

Check insurances

Super funds often include insurance policies: typically life insurance, total and permanent disability insurance and income protection. You may have applied for this cover, or you may have been issued it when you started the account or a new job. The premiums for these insurances are paid out of your super balance, reducing your retirement savings. So it's important to know what you have and to only pay for what you need, while you need it.

Confirm contributions

From July 2025, employers are required to contribute 12 per cent of gross income to their employees' super funds, with payments made each payday. It's a good idea to check that your employer is making regular super contributions.

If you're self-employed, it's up to you to save for your retirement. The earlier you start planning for this and factor it in as a business expense, the better. Some self-employed people contribute a set amount that fits within their cashflow, while others align their contributions with the super guarantee rate that employers must pay their employees. This can be a great starting point.

Update beneficiaries

This is a big one and often overlooked. Unlike your house, car or savings, your superannuation doesn't automatically go to your estate. If you don't nominate a beneficiary for your super fund, the super fund (the trustees) will have discretion over who receives it. Now, that doesn't mean they keep it, or it goes to the government. But it does mean there is room for mistakes, so having a beneficiary is important.

There are two types of nominations

- *Binding nomination:* Your fund must follow your instructions (expires every three years unless non-lapsing).

- *Non-binding nomination:* Your fund considers your wishes but still has discretion over the final decision.

But there are still some restrictions here — and this is where it can get a bit confusing. There are only certain people who qualify to be nominated as beneficiaries. You can nominate:

- your spouse or de facto partner
- your children, including stepchildren and adopted children
- someone financially dependent on you
- your legal personal representative, which sends your super to your estate to be distributed via your will.

But you *can't* directly nominate:

- parents, siblings or friends (unless financially dependent on you)
- your business partner (unless financially dependent on you)
- charities.

If you want your super to go to someone outside the approved list (like a parent, sibling, friend or charity) you can do it by nominating your legal personal representative. This sends your super into your estate, where it will be distributed according to your will. But like most things, this is complicated, and you need advice. This is too important to get wrong, so talk to your super fund, your financial adviser and an estate planning lawyer to make sure you are setting things up the right way.

If you don't nominate correctly, your nomination is invalid, and it's treated as though you don't have one. In this case, your super fund's trustee will decide where your money goes. They are there to do what's in your best interest, but to take out any uncertainty or the risk that your wishes aren't followed, it's important to take some action here.

Make sure these details are up to date to avoid any future headaches or issues!

Reset now: Simplify your super

Let's simplify your super now.

Find your super

First things first: you need to know where your super is.

My superfund is: _____

My current balance is: _____

Locate any lost super

Not sure you know where your super is? It's time to double check!

Login to your myGov account (my.gov.au), head to the ATO portal and you will see a section called 'Super'. Here you will find any records for you.

Check which of these statements applies. myGov has:

☐ multiple funds recorded for me

☐ just the one account for me and it's correct.

Update your super details

Now you know where your super accounts are. Get in contact with the actual super funds directly. The easiest way is to register for their online member portal, but you might need to call them if you have trouble accessing the online platform.

Are all your details correct? Double check details such as birth dates (which often cause lots of headaches).

Check how your super is invested

If you've never actively chosen an investment option, your super is likely in a default setting based on your age.

My super fund is invested in _____ option.

Check if you have insurance

We'll dive deeper into insurance in the next chapter, but for now, just gather the details.

Do I have insurance through super? Circle: Yes / No

The cover I have is _____

The cost of the cover is _____

Check that you are being paid contributions

Has a contribution has been made in the last three months? Circle: Yes / No

No recent contributions? Contact your employer or HR department to clarify when your super will be paid.

Update or add a beneficiary

I have nominated a beneficiary. Circle: Yes / No

My beneficiary is _____

Is it currently a binding or non-binding beneficiary? Circle: Binding / Non-binding

Do I need to update this now? Circle: Yes / No

Are you on track?

Now that you have all the details on where your super is and how much you have, it's common to be thinking, 'Am I on track?' It's a deceptively simple question with a complex answer, because the reality is — there's no single number that fits everyone.

Since we don't have a crystal ball, we have to make an educated guess with the information we do have. In Australia, discussions around how much super is 'enough' often reference benchmarks like those from the Association of Superannuation Funds of Australia (ASFA), which provides a guide based on two lifestyle standards: 'comfortable' or 'modest' retirement standards.

Think of this as a big survey of retired Australians on what they spend each year.

A modest lifestyle covers the essentials (housing, food and bills) while a comfortable lifestyle allows for things such as holidays, dining out and entertainment. But these numbers are general estimates, and the reality is, they might not reflect *your* version of retirement.

This information is handy as it gives us a ballpark estimate of what someone might need, but this doesn't always tell the full story. Here's why:

- *Your lifestyle goals are unique:* These benchmarks assume a specific way of living. If you plan to travel frequently or enjoy a more expensive lifestyle, you'll need more retirement savings.. If you live frugally and have other assets, you might need less.

- *Inflation and rising costs:* The cost of living doesn't stay static and these estimates on inflation can be inaccurate.

- *Healthcare costs are unpredictable:* Anticipating our day-to-day expenses in retirement is hard enough but factoring in unforeseen health costs can be very hard to predict.

- *You may have other income streams:* Super is important, but it's not your *only* option. You might have investment properties, shares, part-time work or other assets funding your retirement.

Personally, I know that looking at the current ASFA standard, 'future Gemma' won't be able to live her best life on the estimated amount per year for a 'comfortable' retirement. She wants to still travel, enjoy her little luxuries and pursue hobbies that bring her joy. But I know plenty of people who could live their best life on that amount.

Instead of relying solely on general benchmarks, you'll need to start with your current budget and adjust it based on what you want your retirement to look like.

Create a retirement budget

To answer if you are on track, you'll need to know what you are aiming to achieve and that means starting with a retirement budget. The easiest way to do this is to get your current budget, the one you created in Chapter 5, and make some changes.

Imagine future you living your best retired life. Ask yourself the following questions and start making some tweaks to your current budget:

- *Housing costs:* Do you plan on owning our own home by then? If so, you'll need to subtract your mortgage or rent; if not, keep those costs in.

- *Education costs:* Will school fees or child-related expenses disappear?

- *Work-related costs:* Consider expenses such as commuting, professional memberships and work attire that may no longer apply.

- *Everyday expenses:* Will grocery, utility or discretionary spending increase or decrease? Some people spend *less* in retirement, but others find they spend *more* once they have extra time for activities, hobbies and socialising.

- *Lifestyle and travel:* How often do you want to travel? What type of travel will you be doing?

- *Big-ticket items:* Do you want to budget for regular car upgrades or home renovations?

- *Healthcare and other unexpected costs:* Do you want a buffer for medical expenses to meet your sleep-at-night test?

Case study: Katie's retirement budget

Katie's current annual budget is $87 000, but that includes several expenses she doesn't expect to have in retirement. She adjusts her budget based on what will stay, go and change:

Current budget: $87 000

- − $35 000 mortgage repayments (her house will be paid off)

- − $8000 school fees (the kids will be independent)

- − $5000 work-related costs (commuting, professional fees, wardrobe)

- + $10 000 overseas travel each year (more time for big trips)

+ $5000 domestic travel each year (more time for weekends away)

+ $10 000 car upgrades (planning to buy a $50 000 car every five years)

+ $10 000 buffer for healthcare and life changes (a buffer to pass her sleep-at-night test)

+ $5200 extra activities and entertainment (more time = more outings)

Estimated retirement budget: $79 200 per year

This process shows that Katie's total spending in retirement won't be much different from now—but how she spends it will shift.

By mapping out these adjustments, you can get a clearer, more realistic idea of your actual retirement needs, rather than relying on generic benchmarks. It won't be perfect, but it's a start, and as you get closer to retirement, this will get more and more accurate.

Reset now: Create your retirement budget

My current budget is $ _____ per year

Areas I will spend more on in retirement that I need to add to my budget

_____

_____

_____

(continued)

Expenses I won't have in retirement that I can subtract from my current budget:

_____

_____

_____

MY CURRENT BUDGET IS (PER YEAR)	$_____
Areas I will spend more on in retirement (add to your budget)	
Housing costs (rent, mortgage if not paid off)	$
Everyday expenses	$
Lifestyle and travel	$
Big-ticket items (one-off costs)	$
Healthcare	$
Unexpected costs	$
Expenses I won't have in retirement that I can subtract from my current budget	
Housing costs (mortgage if paid off)	$
Education costs (school fees)	$
Work-related costs (travel, uniform)	$
Everyday expenses (bills, groceries)	$
Budget + increased expenses = $	
– expenses no longer being paid = $	
Total budget	$

Now you have a rough estimate on what future you might be spending in retirement.

How does your super stack up?

Now that you've got a clearer idea of what your retirement budget might look like, it's time to see how your super stacks up.

Using a retirement calculator is an easy way to estimate how much super you'll need based on your current balance, future contributions and your lifestyle expectations.

A great tool for getting a personalised snapshot is the Moneysmart Retirement Planner calculator (moneysmart.gov.au/retirement-income/retirement-planner). This free tool lets you plug in your actual numbers — your current super balance, expected contributions, age and planned retirement age — and estimate:

- your projected super balance at retirement
- what that balance might look like as yearly income (to compare against what you've estimated you might need).

If you have assets outside of super that you plan to use in retirement, such as a share portfolio, investment property or cash savings, you can include these in your estimate by updating the 'Advanced Setting' section.

It's a good habit to check in on your retirement projections once a year.

Reset now: Stack up your super

Head over to the Moneysmart Retirement Planner and start calculating. Let's take a look:

My total super balance across all funds right now is:

$ _____

Moneysmart calculator projected balance at retirement:

$ _____

My estimated retirement budget:

$ _____ per year

Moneysmart calculator projected income per year in retirement:

$ _____

Make your super work harder and faster

Once you've used the retirement calculator, you should have an idea of how things are looking. If your estimated retirement income looks lower than what you have estimated you will need, don't panic — this is where strategy comes in. Even if you are on track, optimising what you have will always put you in a stronger position.

Just like with your broader finances, there are levers you can pull to improve your financial position, and super is no different. There are a few key adjustments you can make — either individually or combined — to help boost your retirement savings.

That said, super isn't the only way to fund your retirement. In Chapter 12, we'll explore wealth-building strategies outside of superannuation that can help create financial security and flexibility in retirement. But, for now, let's focus on making your super work as hard as possible.

Here are three simple ways to boost your retirement savings:

1. Reduce fees

Super fees quietly eat away at your balance over time, so keeping them in check matters. This doesn't mean going for the absolute cheapest fund, but be aware of what you're paying and make sure it's worth it.

- *Check for multiple accounts:* If you have more than one super fund from past jobs, you could be paying unnecessary duplicate admin fees. Consolidating into one fund (if it makes sense for you) can save money and simplify your admin.

- *Compare investment fees:* The biggest cost in super is usually the fee charged for managing your investments. If your fund's fees are high but performance isn't great, it might be worth looking at other options.

- *Review insurance inside super:* If you have insurance (life, total and permanent disability or income protection) in super, the premiums reduce your balance over time. If you don't need the cover or can get a better deal elsewhere, it's worth reassessing with a qualified adviser who can help you weigh up the pros and cons.

2. Increase performance

How your super is invested makes a huge difference to your future balance. Many people stick with their fund's default investment option, but you have choices.

- *Change your investment strategy:* Super funds offer different investment mixes from conservative (low growth, low risk) to high growth (higher growth potential, higher risk). Depending on your age, time frame to retirement and comfort level, this may be a lever you can pull to increase your retirement savings. Generally, people with a longer time frame to when they will access the money (retirement) will invest more aggressively than people with a shorter time frame. This is because they have more time to ride out any market downturns.

- *Compare fund performance:* Not all super funds perform the same, and they all have different investments and some consistently grow faster than others. Comparing the investment you have in your fund's long-term performance (10+ years) against other funds can help you decide if your money is in the right place, but when comparing you need to make sure you are comparing like-for-like funds. This means looking at investments that have similar asset allocations of shares and also comparing after (net of) fees. If you are unsure, you can call your fund and ask them to help you understand their fees and performance.

For example, I had a client, let's call him Jack, who was 45 when he switched from his fund's default 'balanced' option to a high-growth option. This suited his comfort level and time frame — it passed his sleep-at-night test. With an estimated 1 per cent net return extra each year over 22 years (to age 67), this small tweak could add over $300 000 to his estimated retirement balance.

3. Add more (make contributions)

Adding extra to your super (even small amounts) can massively boost your future retirement savings.

- *Salary sacrifice:* You can direct some of your pre-tax salary into super, reducing your taxable income and growing your balance faster.

- *One-off contributions:* Got a bonus, tax refund or extra savings? Putting even part of it into super can make a big difference over time. You may qualify for a government co-contribution: this is a payment of up to $500 to add into your super when you contribute a certain amount yourself. Or you may be able to have these contributions converted to pre-tax contributions as if they were salary sacrifice, helping you reduce your taxable income while boosting your retirement savings.

- *Catch-up contributions:* If your balance is under $500 000 and you've had years where you couldn't contribute much (e.g., earning less, raising kids, running a business), you might be able to make extra contributions above the standard contribution cap to catch up.

You work hard for your money. Make your contributions work hard for you too.

There are so many ways you can contribute to super, each with different benefits depending on your age and stage. For example, another client, Priya, started contributing just $20 a week into her super bank account via BPAY. Because she is earning under $45 400 and has put in at least $1000 herself, she is eligible for the maximum government co-contribution, which is a top-up of $500 in her super. Free money! Plus, thanks to compound growth, that small tweak could add over $80 000 to her retirement savings by the time she stops working at age 67.

Depending on your income and personal situation, the best way to contribute to super can change year to year. One year, it might make sense to make an after-tax contribution to get the government co-contribution. The next year, if you're earning more, salary sacrificing might be the better move to reduce your taxable income while boosting your super.

To figure out the best option for you each year, try the Moneysmart Super Contributions Calculator (moneysmart.gov.au/grow-your-super/super-contributions-optimiser) — it can help you see which strategy could work best for your situation. And, if you're unsure, talk to your super fund: they can explain the options and help you make an informed decision. And of course, you can always get personal advice from a financial adviser on the best way to maximise your contributions

Where to go for advice

If you've done all you can yourself, or decided *not* to DIY, there are two main ways to get advice about your super:

1. Advisers through your super fund

Many super funds offer access to financial advisers who either work directly for the fund or are closely aligned with it. This is known as *intra-fund advice,* and it's often free or low-cost.

The catch? It's limited in scope. These advisers can help with things like your investment mix, contributions or insurance held within your existing super account, but they generally can't compare different funds or offer broader financial advice beyond the fund's products.

2. Independent financial advisers

An adviser who isn't tied to a specific super fund can take a much broader view. They can help you compare funds, assess fees and performance and make sure your super strategy aligns with your bigger picture — such as retirement plans, your tax strategy and estate planning.

In many cases, some or all of the advice fee can be paid from your super, depending on the type of advice and your fund's rules.

Should you only have one super fund?

You've probably heard that rolling all your super into one fund is the smart move. And, in many cases, it is: fewer accounts mean fewer fees and less admin to keep track of. But here's the catch: *consolidation isn't always the best strategy for everyone.* Sometimes, keeping multiple funds can actually work in your favour.

For example, some funds offer better insurance options than others. If you've got a fund with great insurance that suits your needs, it might be worth keeping, even if you consolidate the rest. Then there's investment choice: different funds have different options.

I have two super funds: one with a minimal amount just to keep the insurances I need, and the other holding the bulk of my super because it offers the right investments for me.

This is why you don't want to jump the gun and consolidate your super without first checking if there's important insurance you might need to keep. Once you consolidate, you lose any existing cover, and that might not be a good move — especially if you'd have trouble getting the same insurance elsewhere or your circumstances have changed. Before making any decisions, take the time to review what's included in your current funds and whether it's worth holding onto.

Should you self-manage your super?

There are multiple different styles of super funds. You're most likely to have heard of industry funds but, on the very opposite scale, there are self-managed super funds (SMSFs).

I find people love the idea of a self-managed super fund before they understand what you can do in a 'normal' fund — and the complications SMSFs can add.

People are drawn to SMSFs because they like the idea of control. These funds allow you to decide exactly how your super is invested, whether that's in property, shares, managed funds or other assets. They also offer potential additional benefits around tax and estate planning.

But, in saying that, given the plot twist that led you to pick up this book may have complicated most areas of your life, throwing an SMSF into the mix might not be the best thing to do. Why? Because running an SMSF isn't as simple as clicking a few buttons. You become the trustee, which means you're responsible for everything: compliance, paperwork, audits and, of course, the actual investing. Yes, you can pay someone to do this for you, but you are still responsible for it.

In my opinion, they suit a minority of people, not the majority. If you think it might be you, you need financial advice and the help of a good accountant to help you weigh up the pros and cons and make that assessment.

Don't set and forget

Superannuation is a long-term strategy, but that doesn't mean you can put it on autopilot. Checking in on your super regularly ensures you stay on track and make informed decisions as your circumstances evolve. Put a recurring reminder in your calendar to check your super once a year, prior to tax time. I think 1 June each year is the perfect time — you still have a full month left of the financial year to act if you need to do anything.

This gives you time to:

- review your super balance and fund performance
- assess how much you've contributed so far in the financial year
- determine the best way to make any additional contributions based on your income and tax benefits before the end of financial year.

Life changes, your spending needs may shift, and inflation will impact your future cost of living. The projections you see today are useful estimates, but they're not set in stone, so they need adjustments over time.

The closer you get to retirement, the more accurate your estimates will be. Regular check-ins help you stay in control, allow you to tweak your strategy as needed and ensure your super remains aligned with your financial goals.

Future you is relying on you to get this right, today.

Chapter 10
Planning for the unexpected

My divorce wasn't the only plot twist that wasn't on my invisible checklist for my life. There were a few plot twists that had made things challenging over the years. One of those plot twists was when my ex-husband stopped working permanently before his 40th birthday due to a medical condition. While this wasn't exactly sudden (he had been living with this medical condition for a while), its progression and impact on our lives — practically, emotionally and financially — certainly had been growing over the years.

Without insurance, the financial fallout of him finishing work because of this condition would have been devastating. I've seen this firsthand with clients too — people forced out of work due to illness or injury, yet still managing to keep their lives moving forward because they had income protection in place. They've gone on to buy homes with home loans, raise kids, go on holidays, all because their insurance policies kept money coming in when their ability to work disappeared.

Life has a way of reminding us that certainty is a luxury we don't always get. Life doesn't stop just because you can't work, and neither should your financial security.

So when navigating a financial reset, it's easy to focus on rebuilding (earning more, managing cashflow and paying down debt), but you must also protect what you're rebuilding.

Insurance and estate planning, such as wills, aren't the most exciting parts of a financial plan, but they are crucial.

We're not getting lost in the overwhelm of policies, legal jargon or 'what if' scenarios in this chapter. Yes, this is important down the track, but we are focusing on what needs to happen right now to safeguard your progress and secure your future. Whether it's reassessing your insurance coverage, updating a will or making sure your financial wishes are clear, this is about putting protection in place without overcomplicating it.

And if you're thinking, 'It won't happen to me', trust me: I've heard that more times than I can count. The reality is, it does happen.

This isn't about fear — it's about being prepared, keeping things simple and ensuring that your future self isn't left scrambling when the unexpected happens.

Protecting what matters

Home, car, pet, private health… the list of 'must have' insurances seems never-ending. I get it — it's another expense. So is personal insurance (also known as life insurance) something you really need?

If you're earning an income, have expenses that you are responsible for, people who depend on you, are working towards your goals and building wealth, I'd say yes — you probably do.

You (and your ability to earn an income) are your biggest asset.

I've lost count of how many times I've met people who insure their $2000 to $10000 car but don't insure their biggest asset — themselves.

So while there are all types of insurances, income protection is one of my non-negotiables, even more so now that I'm single. I am now solely responsible for *all* the expenses in my household and have two little ones depending on me, so I don't have the luxury of taking a chance with it.

Your situation might be different. Maybe you didn't need cover before, or maybe you had some and now need to adjust it based on your current circumstances. We talked about trade-offs and reframing expenses in Chapter 4, and insurance is definitely one expense that needs this approach.

So let's think about it this way. I want you to imagine an employer offered you two options:

- $80000 salary, but if you can't work, you don't get paid

- $75000 salary, but if you're sick or injured, you'll still receive at least 75 per cent of your income until you recover or retire.

When you frame it like this, option 2 is often a no-brainer because you're better off in the long term. In fact, it's a great deal — but it doesn't feel like that when we have to physically pay this to an insurance company as an annual bill.

This example is to help reframe the way we think of insurance — both on the value of cover and what it really costs. Of course, your premium will vary based on your income, occupation, the level of cover you choose and a few personal factors, so it's worth getting proper financial advice. You might find it's a relatively small trade-off for a significant safety net. The key is to have the right cover in place when you need it, but not keep paying for it a day longer than you have to.

Can you afford not to have insurance? Does it pass your sleep-at-night test?

Personal insurances to consider

There are four main types of personal insurance that can protect you and your lifestyle.

1. Life (death) insurance

This type of insurance provides a lump sum payment to your beneficiaries if you pass away. This can help cover living expenses, debts or future costs like your children's education. Some policies also offer a payout while you are still living if you are diagnosed with a terminal illness, and this can help manage medical expenses or give your family options to prepare for the future.

2. Total and permanent disability (TPD) insurance

TPD insurance pays a lump sum if you become permanently disabled and it is unlikely you will work again. This can help cover medical costs, home modifications or lost income. There is generally a waiting period (time off work before it can be paid), which is another reason why an emergency fund is important (see Chapter 2 for more on how to build an emergency fund).

3. Income protection insurance

This insurance replaces a portion of your income (usually up to a max of 85 per cent) if you can't work due to illness or injury. It provides a monthly payment, helping you keep up with bills and maintain your lifestyle while recovering. Like TPD insurance, there is a waiting period for this insurance and also a benefit period (how long you will receive payments for).

4. Trauma insurance (critical illness insurance)

If you're diagnosed with a specific illness such as cancer, heart disease or have a stroke, this insurance will provide you with a lump sum payment. This can help with medical treatment, recovery or simply allow you to take time off work without financial stress. This is the only insurance that isn't offered through your superannuation, so if you haven't set this up yourself and are paying for it out of your own account, then you likely don't have it.

Reset now: Insure your worth!

Do you know which insurances you have?

Do you know what you might actually need?

Compile a list of what insurance you have in super (if any) and any policies outside of super. Fill in the table to get a clearer picture of your coverage and gaps.

(continued)

INSURANCE INSIDE YOUR SUPER		
Life cover	$	
TPD cover	$	Waiting period:
		Benefit period:
Income protection	$	Waiting period:
		Benefit period:
INSURANCE OUTSIDE YOUR SUPER (IF ANY)		
Life cover	$	
TPD cover	$	Waiting period:
		Benefit period:
Income protection	$	Waiting period:
		Benefit period:
Trauma/ critical illness cover	$	Waiting period:
		Benefit period:

Now, ask yourself: is this enough?

My budget right now is $ _____ per month and my income protection covers $ _____ per month.

If I passed away, my family would need a lump sum of $ _____ to cover my debts, be provided for and cover expenses (e.g., funeral).

If I could never work again, I would need a lump sum of $ _____ to cover my debts, possibly buy a suitable home, provide for my family and cover medical expenses.

Where do you stand?

In my experience, when most people look at their insurances, they realise they are not adequately covered.

If that is you, and there's a gap between what you have and what you think you'd need, it's time to get advice. This isn't something you should DIY. There are too many moving parts, and getting it wrong could mean leaving yourself or your family exposed.

Even if you think your bases are covered, at some point, you need to make sure you're not paying more than necessary, and you should check that your policies still align with your needs.

I've seen firsthand how important it is to have the right insurance, and trust me: You want to know well in advance that you have the right cover — not at the time you're hoping to claim on it.

There are two key places to get help with your insurance.

1. Your super fund

Your super fund will likely offer insurance. It's generally a basic, one-size-fits-all option with a single insurer: the one offered by your super fund. You can usually adjust the level of cover, but you can't customise features and benefits.

Your fund can explain what you have and help you increase or decrease your cover, but they won't compare other insurance providers or recommend anything outside of what they offer. That means it might not be the best option for your situation.

2. A financial adviser

My opinion? This should be your plan A.

A financial adviser can help you assess what you actually need and match you with the right policy by comparing multiple insurers. Think of them like a mortgage broker, but for insurance. They can tailor your cover, ensuring you're not paying for features you don't need while still being properly protected. Often, these policies can still be paid through your super fund, but they don't have to be limited to the one insurance provider offered within your fund. You have options. You don't need to be the expert, you just need to recognise when you need help and take the next step.

A *will*ingness for wellness

It's not the most fun topic to discuss, but it's a fact of life: We're not invincible. Estate planning is a crucial part of financial wellness. This becomes even more important when you factor in ageing, health concerns, ex-partners and blended families.

Estate planning isn't just for the wealthy. It's for anyone who wants to make sure they get a say on what happens to their assets.

You might be thinking, *Why would I need a will? I don't have many assets.* But let's pause for a second. Do you have superannuation? Insurance? Even a few sentimental possessions you'd want to go to someone specific? If the answer's yes (and it probably is), then you absolutely need a will. Plus, you're building wealth and working towards your goals, so having an estate plan is essential for safeguarding what you're creating.

Without a clear plan in place, your estate may be handled by legal defaults rather than your wishes. That can mean unnecessary legal fees, frustrating delays and, worst of all, a huge mess for your family to deal with. You may not care, but don't place that burden on them.

Your estate includes everything you own: your property, investments, bank accounts, personal possessions and even your digital assets. Without a plan, the distribution of these assets might not reflect your wishes, creating unnecessary complications, delays and expenses for your loved ones.

There are several key components every estate plan should include:

- *Will:* This essential document outlines how you want your assets distributed and who will care for any minor children. Without a will, the courts make these decisions for you, which may not align with your wishes.

- *Power of attorney:* This designates someone to make financial and legal decisions on your behalf if illness or incapacity prevents you from doing so.

- *Beneficiary designations:* Ensure that accounts with designated beneficiaries (such as life insurance policies and superannuation) are up to date. These designations override instructions in your will, so regular reviews are critical.

Then there are optional extras like:

- *Healthcare directive:* This outlines your preferences for medical treatment if you're unable to communicate them and appoints someone to make healthcare decisions on your behalf.

- *Testamentary trust:* Created through your will, a testamentary trust allows for greater control over the distribution of your assets. It can provide tax benefits, safeguard assets and protect beneficiaries. And it's especially helpful in complex situations such as blended families or young children inheriting wealth.

Estate planning lawyers, financial advisers and tax specialists can help you navigate the process, ensuring your plan is both efficient and effective.

A word on wills

Creating an estate plan can seem daunting. There are so many options on the market it can be hard to work out what steps you should take and who you can turn to for help.

Estate planning can involve complex legal and tax considerations, so consulting professionals is key. Here are some options to consider.

DIY wills

I honestly believe this is not something to DIY. I've seen too many horror stories — wishes scribbled on scraps of paper that people thought counted as a will, over-the-counter will kits that were completed incorrectly or poorly worded documents that created chaos instead of clarity.

Yes, a DIY will feels like a quick win: cheap, easy and off your to-do list. But the risks are huge. If it isn't signed or witnessed correctly, it may not be legally valid. Ambiguous wording can lead to family disputes or assets ending up in the wrong hands. This is one area where getting it right is critical.

Online will platforms

For those looking for a middle ground between DIY and expert advice, an online will platform can be a useful option. These services, when created by lawyers, help streamline the process and reduce costs. They can work well for simple, straightforward estates where there are no complexities, such as blended families, multiple assets, family conflicts or dependants with special needs.

This might be the right solution for now, but as your life changes and your estate grows, it's worth reassessing whether a more comprehensive approach is needed. When things get more complicated, getting expert advice is essential.

Government services

In Australia, public trustee services in some states offer free or low-cost will-drafting options. It is a basic solution but may be appropriate for some situations.

A common myth is that you *must* appoint the public trustee as the executor to use the service. You don't. That's where many of the costs start to creep in, so it's important to understand your options.

Estate planning lawyer

My recommendation to most people, even those without overly complex situations, is that they should be getting personal advice with an estate planning specialist. In my experience, this professional advice is worth every cent. It's not just about the paperwork. It's about getting the right guidance on what you can and can't do — and more importantly, what you should do.

A lawyer ensures your estate is structured properly, protects assets and prevents nasty surprises for your loved ones. They can also determine if you should have things like testamentary trusts, which provide asset protection, and power of attorney, which ensures someone you trust can make financial or medical decisions on your behalf if you are unable to.

Peace-of-mind protocols

Estate planning might not be the most exciting task on your to-do list, but it's one of the most important. It's about making sure your wishes around money and assets will be carried out the way you want — not left for the courts to decide. Below are three golden rules for peace of mind.

1. Get onto it sooner, not later

People often put off estate planning because it feels overwhelming, or they think they have plenty of time. In my experience, life throws curveballs when we least expect it. Procrastination can leave your loved ones in a tough spot, with no clear plan to follow. The best time to start is now: Even a simple plan is better than no plan.

2. Keep it simple, but personal

Some people create such overcomplicated plans it takes years to unravel! On the flip side, some people create a plan but make it overly basic, thinking, *This should cover everything*. But life isn't that straightforward. Your assets, family dynamics and personal wishes all need to be considered. A cookie-cutter approach might leave gaps, causing confusion or disputes later. Taking the time to personalise your plan ensures it truly reflects your values and priorities.

3. Include digital assets

In today's world, our digital lives hold a surprising amount of value — financially, emotionally and practically. Yet so many people forget to include digital assets in their estate plans. From social media accounts to online banking and even cryptocurrency, these need to be addressed. Without a plan, your loved ones could face major headaches trying to access or manage these.

If you haven't left clear instructions, your loved ones will have to pick up the pieces — and that's not fair to them.

Reset now: Weigh up your will and worth

Take a moment to revisit the work you did on your net worth in Chapter 1.

Look at your assets: your home, investments, savings and super.

- If something happened to me, who would these assets go to?

- Who is the nominated beneficiary for my superannuation?

- Who would receive my life insurance payout?

- Are there any special wishes I want to account for in my estate plan?

Do you have a will?

My will is located: _____

Who knows the location of my will: _____

Has a significant event happened since I last updated it (e.g., marriage, divorce, kids, major asset changes)? Is my will still aligned with my wishes?

If the answer is no or that it's outdated, then it's time for action!

Are things straightforward?

If yes, list at least one estate planning lawyer you will call to ask about your options, their recommendations based on your situation and how much it will cost. It can't hurt to make sure they agree your situation is straightforward.

Lawyer option 1: _____

If no, list two estate planning lawyers you will call to ask about your options, their recommendations based on your situation and how much it will cost.

Lawyer option 1: _____

Lawyer option 2: _____

Pick your next step:

☐ DIY (please no!)

☐ online

☐ public trustee

☐ government services

☐ estate planning lawyer

Don't file away and forget

Once you've got your estate plan sorted, don't just file it away and forget about it. Life changes (marriage, divorce, kids, new assets), so your plan should evolve too.

Make it a habit to check in on your estate plan every couple of years or whenever a major shift happens. And while estate planning isn't exactly light conversation, having an open chat with your family can save a lot of stress down the track. A little clarity now can prevent confusion later, making sure your wishes are understood and your loved ones are looked after exactly as you intend.

And, most importantly, make sure someone knows where to find your will and any key documents when the time comes.

The best estate plan is one that can actually be put into action.

Chapter 11

Protecting your financial future

Money is often one of the biggest sources of conflict in relationships, yet it's rarely just about dollars and cents. It's about values, security, freedom and even identity. Couples don't enter relationships as blank slates when it comes to money. They bring their own habits, beliefs and emotional baggage, which are often shaped during childhood and reinforced over time. And when two people merge their financial lives, those differences don't just disappear.

Money conflicts in relationships often go far deeper than spending habits or savings goals. They touch on autonomy, security, fairness and long-term priorities. They reveal how each partner was raised to think about money, what they fear and what they value. Without open and ongoing communication, even the best-intentioned financial arrangements can create tension.

Take a couple like Lauren and Ben. When they first moved in together, money seemed like a non-issue. Ben had always been relaxed about finances—he saw money as a tool to enjoy life, a way to make the everyday more comfortable. Lauren, on the other hand, was meticulous. She tracked every dollar, planned for the future and felt uneasy if their bank account dipped below a certain number. They both contributed to expenses, but over time, their different approaches began to cause friction. Lauren felt like she was the only one thinking ahead, while Ben resented the restrictions she placed on spontaneous spending. The deeper issue? They had never talked about their expectations, their financial goals or what security meant to them individually.

Then there's Jason and Mia. From the outside, their financial setup looked seamless. Jason handled everything, from paying the bills to managing investments, and Mia trusted him completely, happy to let him take the lead. That was, until a family emergency forced her to step in. Suddenly, she realised she had no idea how their finances worked, where their money was invested or even what their financial position truly was. What started as a practical division of responsibilities had left her financially vulnerable.

Whether you're two months into a relationship or 20 years in, building a healthy financial dynamic as a couple is essential.

Getting money relationships right

Just like resetting your personal finances, it's never too late to change how you approach money together. The three things that make money relationships healthy are:

1. Your own relationship with money

Your mindset, your habits, your values: These are the foundations of how you approach money, and they don't just disappear when you enter a relationship. We've already done the deep work in

Chapter 1, stripping back old patterns and redefining what truly matters. Now, the challenge is staying true to that.

It's easy to get caught up in a new relationship and start to compromise on financial values in the name of love, to slip into old habits or adopt someone else's approach just to avoid conflict. But real financial independence doesn't mean keeping everything separate, it means knowing who you are, what you need and holding onto that, even in a partnership.

2. Communication as a couple

When two people come together, they each bring their own money story—how they were raised, their experiences with finances and what money represents to them. If you don't talk about it early and often, those differences can turn into tension fast.

Open and honest conversations about money are so important. It's not about merging finances or having the same money habits. It's about understanding each other, respecting different approaches and figuring out how to work as a team. The best relationships aren't about two people agreeing on everything; they're about two people learning how to navigate differences together.

And timing matters. The middle of a fight over money is *not* the time to start discussing finances. Instead, set aside time when you're both calm and open, whether that's regular 'money dates' or just a casual check-in over coffee. Talk about where you're at, where you want to be and how you can support each other in getting there.

Most importantly, approach these conversations with curiosity, not judgement. Your partner's money habits aren't a personal attack; they're shaped by years of experiences you haven't lived.

The more you listen and understand, the easier it becomes to build a financial future that works for both of you. Remember, you are a team!

3. Managing money independently as well as together

One big misconception I see all the time is that love means merging everything, including your bank accounts. But let me be clear: Being in a partnership doesn't mean you have to merge finances. There's no rule book that says working towards a shared life and financial objectives requires merged bank accounts. Do what feels right for you.

Whether you decide to keep your finances separate, blend them together or adopt a hybrid approach, the focus should always be on what aligns with your comfort levels and relationship dynamics. As your relationship grows and changes, let your financial strategies evolve with it.

What does that look like in practice? Here are three common scenarios that can work.

1. The 50/50 approach

This method involves splitting expenses evenly, with each person paying half. Some couples stick to a strict 50/50 split, while others take turns covering costs, keeping things balanced overall. This can work well if both partners have similar incomes and resources; however, if one person earns significantly less, it can create an unfair burden and lead to tension.

2. Percentage allocation

If there's a big difference in income or assets, splitting everything equally might not feel fair. The percentage approach adjusts each partner's contribution based on what they earn. This ensures both people are contributing proportionally, creating a more balanced and equitable financial arrangement.

For example, let's say your household expenses are $4000 per month. Partner A earns $6000 per month and Partner B earns $4000. Instead of splitting the expenses 50/50 ($2000 each), you could use a percentage-based approach. Partner A earns 60% of the total income, so they contribute 60% of the expenses ($2400); Partner B, earning 40%, contributes $1600. This way, both partners are contributing fairly in proportion to their earnings.

3. Parallel finance

Some couples keep things completely separate, each handling their own finances while contributing in different ways that feel right for them. This might mean taking it in turns paying for things or each person being responsible for different expenses.

The key is to find a system that works for both of you — one that feels fair and equitable, while staying flexible enough to evolve. As life changes, so do your financial dynamics. Scenarios such as kids from previous relationships, living in a home one partner owns or one person stepping into an unpaid homemaker role can all add layers of complexity. What feels balanced today might not feel the same in five or ten years, so keeping the conversation open and being adaptable is essential.

It's important that each person retains a sense of independence and ownership. While you don't both need to be managing the day-to-day (and sometimes boring) tasks like paying the bills (because this often naturally falls to one person), it's still crucial that both of you understand what's happening with your finances and have access and oversight.

One of my favourite sayings is: *You can outsource the execution but not the understanding.* That applies to your finances in a relationship, and it also applies to your adviser, accountant or any other professional in your life. You need to be aware of where your money is and what it is doing.

Reset now: Prepare for your future

Use this as an opportunity to reflect on what a healthy financial relationship looks like for you, whether you're navigating one now or preparing for the future.

Take some time to reflect on how money is (or would be) managed in your relationship and whether your current approach aligns with what you want.

If you're in a relationship

Current approach: How do you and your partner currently handle money? Are finances merged, separate or a mix of both?

_____

_____

Evolution: Has your approach changed over time? If yes, what triggered the change?

_____

_____

Effectiveness: Is your current system working well for both of you? Does it feel fair and balanced?

_____

_____

Adaptability: Have there been any life changes (e.g., kids, career shifts, homeownership, unpaid caregiving) that might require a new approach?

_____

_____

Future adjustments: If your financial system isn't working as well as it could, what small changes could you make to improve it?

_____

_____

If you're single

Past experiences: How have you handled money in past relationships? What worked and what didn't?

_____

_____

_____

Your preferences: In a relationship, would you prefer to keep finances separate, merge them or find another balance?

_____

Non-negotiables: What financial values and habits are most important to you in a future partner?

_____

_____

_____

(continued)

Adaptability: How might your financial approach shift during different life stages (e.g., living together, starting a family, career changes)?

_____

_____

_____

Future planning: What steps can you take now to build financial confidence and independence before entering a new relationship?

_____

_____

_____

To prenup or not?

In Australia, the idea of a prenup isn't as common as it is in the US, but we have something similar: binding financial agreements (BFAs). BFAs are legal documents that outline what each person brings to the relationship and how assets may be divided if things don't work out. Not exactly romantic, I know, but neither is dealing with financial fallout if a relationship ends unexpectedly.

This isn't about expecting the worst; it's about being a team, a partnership and protecting both of you. When emotions are high at the start of a relationship, financial protection might not feel urgent, but down the track, things can get complicated — especially when factors such as children, business ownership or significant assets are involved. A BFA is a framework. It draws a line in the sand and creates a clear plan.

There's also the legal side of things. In Australia, you're typically considered a de facto couple under Family Law after two years of living together, but that's not a hard and fast rule. Other factors, such as getting married, financially contributing to each other's lives or having a child together, can impact that time frame and your legal rights. If you're in a serious relationship, getting legal advice early on can save a lot of stress later.

At the end of the day, money in relationships isn't about rules or one-size-fits-all approaches. It's about making informed decisions that support both your financial independence and your shared goals.

You don't *have* to merge finances to build a strong relationship. You don't *have* to buy a house together to feel financially secure. And you don't *have* to follow the traditional path just because that's what others expect.

What matters is that you and your partner are on the same page, communicating openly, respecting each other's financial choices and building a future that works for *both* of you. When money is handled well, it becomes a tool that strengthens your relationship, not something that drives a wedge.

Taking steps to protect yourself means building a relationship based on transparency, mutual respect and security so both of you know you're making smart choices for now and for the future.

Raising money-smart kids

By now you know that money isn't just about numbers. It's shaped by beliefs, habits and the stories we've absorbed over a lifetime, so we should also be thinking about our impact on the next generation.

The way we were raised influences how we think about money and, in turn, the way we talk to the next generation shapes *their* financial future. While we can't go back and rewrite our own childhood money lessons, we *can* break cycles and start having better, more open conversations — ones that empower the next generation to make confident financial choices.

Imagine if, as kids, we had more open, practical conversations about money. How might that have shaped our financial confidence today? While we can't change the past, we *can* choose to do things differently moving forward.

Whether it's your kids, grandkids, nieces, nephews or any young person close to you, they are *always* watching and absorbing the attitudes and habits of the adults around them. And in times of big life changes, such as separation, job loss or the passing of a loved one, our financial behaviours become even more visible. During these transitions, it's natural to want to protect and provide for our kids, but it's equally important to teach them the skills to stand on their own two feet.

A common consideration for parents is whether we should *save* for our kids or teach them *self-reliance*. The answer depends entirely on your financial situation and what values you want to instil. The goal isn't just to give them money. It's to equip them with the knowledge and confidence to navigate their own financial journey.

You can't support others if you're struggling yourself. If you're not in a position to save or invest for your kids right now, that's okay. You can still have a powerful impact on their financial literacy without spending a cent.

Securing your own financial wellbeing first isn't selfish — it's necessary. Like airplane safety, you must put your own oxygen mask on first.

Teaching kids about money doesn't have to be complicated. It's often the small, everyday (age appropriate) conversations that leave the biggest impact:

- *Lead by example:* Kids learn from what we do, not just what we say. Show them how you plan your expenses, save for goals and make mindful money decisions.

- *Make money a normal conversation:* Talk about why we work, how money is earned and where it goes. The more open we are, the less intimidating these concepts become.

- *Differentiate wants from needs:* Use everyday situations, such as grocery shopping or online browsing, to highlight the difference between wants and needs.

- *Involve them in decisions:* Let them help compare prices, work out change at the shops or set a small savings goal. Real-life experience is the best teacher.

- *Frame money in a positive way:* Instead of 'we can't afford that', try 'we're choosing to spend our money on x right now'. It shifts the mindset from scarcity to intentional choices.

By making these lessons part of everyday life, we help kids grow into financially confident adults — something far more valuable than any trust fund or savings account.

Mum's the word

While we focus so much on shaping the financial habits of the next generation, there's another side to this conversation: talking about money with *our* parents and grandparents. And let's be honest, this can be a much harder conversation to have.

For many people (from older generations or not!), money can be a private matter. It's not something that is often openly discussed, but as we get older, money conversations become more important — especially when it comes to ensuring financial security in retirement and making sure our wishes are understood and respected.

Talking about money with older family members should never be about control, it should be about understanding what's important to them, making sure they're financially secure and avoiding unnecessary stress down the track. The reality is, without these conversations, families often find themselves scrambling to make big financial decisions *for* their loved ones without really knowing what they wanted.

I've seen so many different scenarios play out:

- Parents who won't spend on themselves in retirement because they feel they *should* leave an inheritance — even at the cost of their own comfort and security.

- Older family members who won't ask for financial help, even when a small change could massively improve their quality of life.

- A complete lack of planning: outdated wills, no clear estate plan or important documents that no one knows about until it's too late.

Avoiding these conversations doesn't stop tough financial situations from happening; it just makes them harder to navigate when they do.

At the heart of these conversations is the idea of *legacy* — and this isn't just about what's left behind in a bank account. It's about the financial habits, attitudes and values that get passed down through generations.

One of the biggest challenges I see with inheritance is the *emotional* side of it. I've had so many conversations with people who have inherited money and suddenly feel guilt, pressure or a deep responsibility to use it in a way they think would honour their loved one's wishes. This can lead to two extreme reactions: either spending the money quickly and impulsively *or* holding onto it so tightly that it remains untouched out of fear of making the 'wrong' decision.

If an inheritance may be part of your financial future, the first rule is this: Don't rely on it as your future safety net.

Life is unpredictable. Health issues, unexpected costs or changing circumstances can quickly shift what was once a 'guaranteed' inheritance. Making financial decisions based on an assumed windfall is risky at best.

However, if you do receive an inheritance, taking a thoughtful approach can turn it into a powerful tool for long-term financial security. Instead of making quick decisions, take the time to step back and think about how this money can be used to align with *your* values, goals and future plans.

How to start the conversation

Unless it's figuring out how to reset the TV, log in to Netflix or troubleshoot their phone, our parents and grandparents aren't often big on asking for help. When it comes to money, health or life's bigger challenges, our family members often prefer to figure things out on their own — even if it means struggling in silence.

You can't force someone to talk about their finances, but you *can* approach it in a way that encourages open and respectful discussion.

- *Pick the right time.* Bringing up estate planning in the middle of Sunday lunch? Probably not ideal. Instead, find a quiet moment where they feel comfortable and in control of the conversation.

- *Lead with empathy.* Frame it around their wishes, not the financial details. It's about making sure their plans are in place, not about what they're leaving behind. Sometimes it can be helpful to frame it in the context of a past experience they may have had dealing with the loss of a loved one.

- *Listen without judgement.* Even if you don't agree with their views, acknowledging their perspective is key to keeping the conversation open.

Offer support, not pressure. If they're unsure about where to start, suggest speaking with a financial adviser or estate planner to make sure everything is in place. Keep in mind, you may not be the person they feel most comfortable talking to this about and you need to be okay with that.

Open and honest conversations help families avoid misunderstandings, prevent financial mismanagement and ensure that wealth, whether in the form of money or knowledge, is passed down in a way that genuinely benefits future generations.

Talking about money (across all generations) is how we break the cycle of silence and create real change.

Pass it on

As you reflect on all the work you've done throughout this journey in resetting your mindset and your habits, refocusing on your financial foundations and redefining what financial security looks like, consider how you can share that knowledge with those around you.

The more we normalise these discussions, the more we empower not just ourselves and our partners, but also our parents, children and grandchildren to navigate money with confidence, independence and ease.

The real gift is passing on a healthier, open approach to money, so those closest to us can also stand on stronger financial ground.

Chapter 12

Finding freedom in flexibility

Now that you've reset your mindset, optimised your cashflow, tackled debt and safeguarded your finances, it's time to think bigger. Financial security isn't just about covering the basics. It's about building a life with real choices. It's the ability to pivot, adapt and move forward with confidence, no matter what life throws at you.

Financial freedom is often seen as the ultimate goal — a huge milestone that sits at the end of the road, waiting to be reached. A big, round number. A final destination. But is it really?

For many people, *financial freedom* is something they often add to their invisible checklist of success. The final destination to aim for. I know did.

A quick Google search will throw you into a whirlwind of early retirement stories, passive income formulas and calculators promising to reveal your *magic number*. You'll find hacks, strategies and bold claims of how to escape the grind forever. It's a rabbit hole — one filled with tales of extreme frugality, unexpected wins, crushing setbacks and inspiration that either fires you up or leaves you wondering if you've already missed the boat.

And while it's a great goal to aspire to, right now, if you're resetting, refocusing and, ultimately, rebuilding, that kind target might feel overwhelming. And that's okay.

The other issue with treating that magic number like a final destination is that the number is always changing. *We* change. *Life* changes. As we grow, our priorities shift. As we have more, we get used to more and often want more. It's a moving target as life evolves. What seemed like 'enough' five years ago might not feel the same today.

That's why fixating on a single number can be tricky, especially when you don't yet know what your life will look like down the track. Right now, your focus should be on taking steps that create freedom in different areas of your life today.

It might be the freedom to get some breathing room in your budget. The freedom to say no to work that drains you. The freedom to build skills that will open up new income streams. The freedom to make financial decisions with confidence instead of fear. The freedom of choice in the future.

Financial freedom shouldn't mean waiting until you have a certain amount of money before you start living. It's actually about *building financial flexibility* so you can create options, security and independence as you go, not just when you hit that magic number.

Right now, you don't need to have the perfect plan for *total* financial freedom. You just need to focus on the next step — making intentional moves that bring you more control, more opportunities and more confidence in your financial future.

Financial freedom shouldn't be a finish line. It's a journey of self-discovery and that means being flexible.

Being financially flexible

To create financial flexibility, yes, you need to build wealth because *wealth is what creates choice*, and that doesn't happen by accident. That's what this stage is about — not focusing on a magic number, but *moving forward*, so that whatever your future vision looks like, you're already on the path to making it happen.

Your ability to build assets (whether that's shares, super, property or business income) comes from making intentional money moves now. That includes:

- using surplus income wisely instead of letting lifestyle creep absorb it

- paying down debt, so more of your income can go towards wealth-building

- increasing your income to give you more financial power

- investing, so your money works for you instead of sitting stagnant.

The thought of investing can be daunting if you haven't thought too much about it before, but it doesn't need to be. Chances are you are already an investor thanks to your superannuation.

The secret sauce for investing is compound interest. Just like superannuation, which we talked about in Chapter 9, the power of investing lies in regular contributions over a long period and, largely, the heavy lifting done by compound interest.

Compounding is how wealth snowballs over time. It's the process of earning returns not just on your initial investment but also on the returns *that* investment generates. In simple terms? Your money starts making money, and then that money makes even more money. The earlier you start, the more powerful compounding becomes — because *time* is the secret ingredient.

Imagine investing $10 000 with a 7 per cent return. In one year, you earn $700, but in year two, you're earning 7 per cent on $10 700 (which increases your new total to $11 449). That's how small gains turn into serious wealth over time.

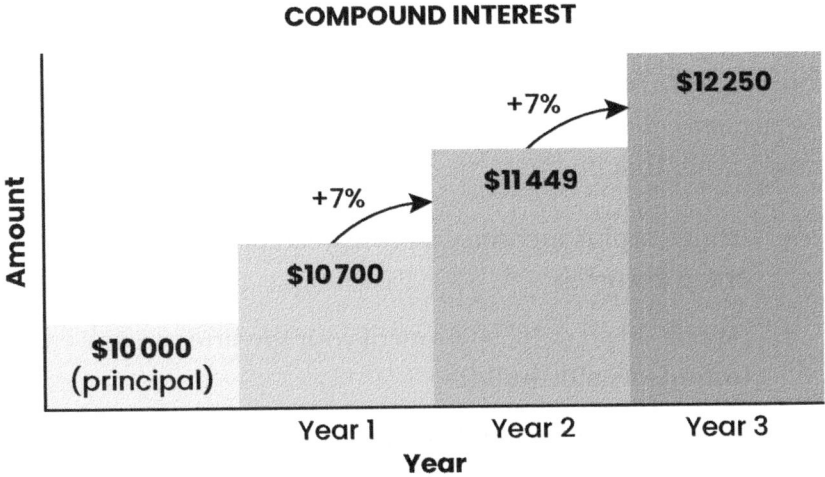

COMPOUND INTEREST

Whether it's your main game plan or part of a bigger strategy, optimising your super is a smart move, but super is just one piece of the puzzle for you. It's a long-term asset that works alongside other assets in a broader strategy.

Adding more assets outside of super gives you even more control and allows you to access financial flexibility at different stages.

Building other assets

There are two main types of assets that help build wealth.

1. Growth assets

Growth assets increase in value over time. The goal is capital growth: buying something that appreciates so you can sell it later for more than you paid. Think of things like shares (stocks), property and businesses. These assets don't always provide immediate cashflow, but they have the potential for significant long-term gains.

A simple example is that you buy a house for $500 000, its value increases, and you sell it when it's worth $700 000. That's a $200 000 gain.

With shares, the same concept applies. Say you buy a share for $5, and its value increases. You sell it when it's worth $7 per share, meaning you've made $2 profit per share.

2. Income assets

Income assets generate ongoing income that you can use to support your lifestyle or reinvest for further growth. Examples include bonds, dividend-paying shares and rental-property income from businesses. These assets provide regular cashflow.

Using the property example again: Let's say the house is worth $500 000, but instead of purely relying on it to grow in value, you rent it out. That rental income might cover expenses while you wait for the property to appreciate, or it could provide extra cash to fund your lifestyle. Or both.

Similarly, some shares pay dividends (regular payments to shareholders). This means you're receiving income from your investment without having to sell it. Even if the share price doesn't increase, you're still making money.

While you're working, you might prioritise growth assets to build wealth, but when you retire, income assets might take centre stage to fund your lifestyle.

Then, there are also assets that build both growth and income. A well-chosen investment property might grow in value *and* generate rental income. Some shares increase in price *and* pay dividends.

The key is understanding what role each asset plays in your financial strategy — whether it's focused on growth, income or a mix of both — and being flexible as your needs change. Getting the right balance is what ultimately gives you financial security, flexibility and freedom of choice.

Let's now explore how you can build financial flexibility through different assets and strategies, so you can start shaping a path that works for you.

How to make it work for you

The beauty of building wealth is that it doesn't have to follow a traditional script. You can craft a path that resonates with your life goals and circumstances. Whether through property, investments, a business or a combination of these, the most important factor is that your strategy works for you.

Remember, there's no one right way to build wealth, only the way that aligns with your vision for your life.

To understand how this works in practice, we'll look at real stories of how people have built financial flexibility in their lives: what assets they used, how they structured their finances and the different ways they created options for themselves.

Case study: The health curveball

Ravi had a stable career he loved and, for the most part, life was ticking along nicely for him, until, at age 50, he was forced to take six months off due to a medical condition. When he returned, he could only work three days a week for several years, reducing his income significantly. His employer continued making minimum super contributions, but with his lower income, this resulted in $4500 less being added to his super each year.

Ravi's priority was to reduce his home loan, aiming to remain on track to be debt-free by retirement. To achieve this, he reset his expenses, cutting unnecessary costs, while factoring in added medical expenses.

When he was able to return to full-time work, Ravi was already used to living on a reduced income. He used this to his advantage, maintaining his new cost of living and directing all his surplus income towards extra super contributions and accelerating his home loan repayments.

Ravi's financial flexibility

By the time he retired at 65, he owned his home outright and had just over $400 000 in his super. He drew $50 000 per year in income from his super to cover his living expenses from 65 to 67.

Qualifying for an age pension at 67 meant Ravi didn't need to draw as much from his super each year, stretching his balance further and ensuring his lifestyle could be maintained well into his 90s. He also has the added financial flexibility of downsizing his home in the future, if needed.

Key takeaways

A health setback could have derailed Ravi's retirement plans, but by cutting costs, adjusting his goals and working with a money coach and adviser, he stayed on track. Living below his means gave him the flexibility to rebuild and retire debt-free.

Case study: The property pivot

Sarah and Amal bought a home in their early 30s and, a few years later, purchased their first investment property using the equity from their home for the deposit.

By their late 40s, their first investment property had increased in value, and they were able to, once again, use equity to purchase another investment property. Rental income covered most of the investment properties' costs, and they topped up the shortfall from their salaries.

However, when interest rates increased, they were struggling to make ends meet with three mortgages, which left them feeling uneasy (it didn't pass their sleep-at-night test).

Amal and Sarah decided to reduce their debt so they could add more of what they loved into their life today, while balancing long-term investing.

Amal and Sarah's financial flexibility

Amal and Sarah decided to sell their primary residence and move into one of their investment properties. They used the sale proceeds to clear the outstanding debt on the property they moved into and hold an emergency fund of $50 000 to pass their sleep-at-night test. They also started investing in super and a personal share portfolio to diversify their wealth.

Key takeaways

When juggling three mortgages became too much, Sarah and Amal reassessed their priorities. With guidance from their adviser, accountant and real estate agent, they sold a property to reduce debt and created a simpler, more sustainable strategy. This freed up cashflow for today while still building wealth for the future, just at a pace that felt more manageable for them.

Case study: The entrepreneur's edge

Mei had always been entrepreneurial. In her early 30s, she started a business. Initially she was barely able to cover a wage for herself, let alone pay herself superannuation. Her business expenses were lean, and she was also keeping her living expenses low, sharing a rental with a friend.

She was confident in her business and her ability to make it work. Within five years she was drawing a regular income from the business and started paying herself super at the government-mandated percentage.

Several years later, her business needed a premises. She decided to buy a commercial property via a self-managed super fund that her business leased from the super fund. She remained renting where she lived and felt being a long-term renter suited her lifestyle. Her focus was on the business, and she reinvested the profits back into the business. She was happy to have some diversification outside the business, with the commercial property and her super now growing.

Mei's financial flexibility

By her late 50s, Mei had built a valuable company with steady recurring revenue. She also had the commercial property within her superannuation fund, which had grown substantially in value. She had lots of choices, including:

- sell the business and property,

- sell one and keep the other asset for income, and/or
- step back from full-time work.

Selling one or both of these assets meant, when she was ready, she could buy a house in retirement keeping remaining funds for lifestyle and living costs.

Key takeaways

Mei prioritised building her business in the early years, keeping expenses low and backing herself. She leaned on her village of support people and, with the help of trusted professionals, made strategic decisions, such as investing through super and reinvesting profits. This gave her long-term financial flexibility and multiple options for retirement, all without owning a home along the way.

Case study: The lifestyle leap

Jamie's financial world turned upside down overnight when their spouse passed away. Jamie's partner left behind a small super balance and a life insurance policy of $200 000.

After spending years focused on raising their three children and working part time on and off, now at the age of 45, they found themselves a solo parent re-entering full-time work.

When Jamie returned to work, they used $100 000 they had remaining from the life insurance policy as a deposit for a family home, which used a significant portion of the family finances. With their expenses already as tight as was practical, Jamie focused on the levers they had: increasing income by upskilling and advancing their career.

Jamie's financial flexibility

At 60, Jamie's children had moved out of the family home and were all living in different states in Australia. Jamie still had a mortgage, but was ready for a new adventure. Jamie had options:

- keep the house and rent it out to cover the mortgage,
- downsize the property to lower the mortgage, or
- downsize to have no mortgage entirely, leaving them debt-free.

Jamie decided to sell the home to clear the mortgage, buy a campervan and live a nomadic lifestyle, discovering Australia. Within six months of being on the road, Jamie met someone. They travelled together, each in their own motorhomes but sharing life and experiences. They eventually fell in love again — this time with a small beachside town where they bought a house together to call home.

Key takeaways

Jamie faced a major life shift after losing their partner, stepping into full-time work while raising three children solo. With the support of their village, plus a professional money coach and a financial adviser, Jamie focused on career growth and made intentional financial choices: building stability and keeping their future flexible.

By age 60, Jamie had the means to buy a smaller, more suitable home on their own, but after meeting someone on the road, they chose to build a life together — not out of necessity, but from a place of strength and independence.

And last, but in no way least, this is the true story of an amazing person who is still well and truly in the thick of rebuilding their finances and their life, but is one of the most inspiring people I have ever met.

Case study: The last victim

At 40, Tracy Hall found herself a single mum, navigating life after divorce and embracing new opportunities. Tracy was getting on top of her finances while navigating her divorce, she had a solid career (superannuation was looking good) and she was feeling confident about her future and excited to dip her toe into the world of dating.

Tracy met a man, fell in love and built a solid relationship made up of family holidays, plans for the future and a bond built on mutual respect and aligned values. After almost 18 months in this new relationship, Tracy discovered she had been a victim of a serial con artist. The man she fell in love with was not who he said he was. Over $300 000 of her superannuation and savings were gone. The financial and emotional devastation was overwhelming, and Tracy lost faith in her ability to make the right decisions. She knew she couldn't rebuild alone.

Determined to take back control and build a future she deserved, she carefully assembled the people she needed in her village — one of whom was a trusted financial adviser. With the financial adviser's guidance, she went to work optimising her income, maximising her super contributions, saving as much as she could and building new investment strategies.

Key takeaways

Through resilience, smart financial moves and the support of her village, Tracy didn't just recover, she's now in a stronger financial position than ever — and she's not stopping there. Tracy is using her experience to help others safeguard their finances and take control of their own financial futures.

Tracy's story is a powerful reminder that setbacks don't define you — how you rise from them does. You can read about Tracy's amazing comeback story in her book, *The Last Victim*.

Find what works for you

Each of these examples highlights something important: Financial flexibility looks different for everyone.

Some people rely on a single asset type, while others build multiple streams of income. Some aim for early retirement, while others want the ability to work on their own terms. Some focus on passive income, while others prefer growing assets they can cash in later.

There's no perfect formula, only *what works for you*. The key takeaway? You don't have to wait for the 'perfect' strategy before you start. The goal is to *begin building wealth now*, so that whatever your future looks like, you have options.

Start imagining

It can be hard to imagine what life might look like in 12 months, let alone ten years.

But while not knowing can be uncertain and scary, it can also be *exciting*. That uncertainty doesn't have to be overwhelming. It can be empowering. That's why I don't currently have a fixed wealth target I'm working towards. Yes, loosely, I have a plan (I'm still a financial adviser after all), but what I am doing is working towards being *happier, healthier and wealthier* in everyday steps.

I'm building assets so that when I decide what my future looks like, *I have the financial foundation to support it*. I've optimised my super, and with the spare cashflow I've worked into my budget, I'm steadily building a share portfolio to provide flexibility and income. At the same time, I'm growing a property portfolio for long-term wealth. I'm doing what I can with the resources I have.

I don't own a family home, and right now, it's not a priority. As someone who has recently divorced, I don't yet know what *my version* of family will look like in the future. Renting suits me and my kids *for now*. While at this stage of my journey I cannot imagine meeting someone I want to combine my finances and life with, that may change. Maybe one day I'll buy a home with a new partner, and we'll create a beautiful blended-family home together. Or maybe I'll decide I'm ready for solo homeownership on my own terms and buy something perfect for just me and the kids. Either way, I know *I'll need assets to fund whatever choice I make*.

So even without knowing the final destination (my ultimate financial freedom goal), I'm working towards *financial flexibility* every day, and you can too.

We can still make intentional decisions—putting as much as we can (within our budget) towards creating options, while also making sure we are enjoying life today.

Reset now: Imagine what life could be

List all the ways life might change for the better in the future that you would want to allow flexibility for. For example, would you like to travel the world, buy a new home with a partner, live in another country or take a career break?

1. _____

2. _____

3. _____

Which assets (growth assets such as property, income through shares or a mix of both) do you have now that might help with your ideal future scenario?

1. _____

2. _____

3. _____

Who in your village can help you achieve these future goals?

1. _____

2. _____

3. _____

We've explored what financial flexibility looks like. And you've identified how your financial future might evolve, the assets that could support you and the intentional moves that will create more security and choice in your life.

But here's the key takeaway: You don't need all the answers right now. What matters is that you've built the ability to adapt, pivot and move forward with confidence no matter what life throws your way.

Financial flexibility isn't about reaching a final destination. It's about creating options, shaping a future that works for *you* and making decisions that align with your evolving goals. You don't have to wait for the 'perfect moment', or even know what 'perfect' looks like just yet to start living the life you want.

Now, let's bring it all together by revisiting your 12-step plan. Take a moment to reflect on each of the steps on the opposite page. How have these steps already changed your financial future? Which ones have had the greatest impact so far on your path forward? You might feel you've made it to step 12 (financial flexibility) already, or there might be some steps you want to revisit soon. Remember: Your money reset is at your own pace. The important thing is to keep moving forward.

Your 12-Step Money Reset Plan

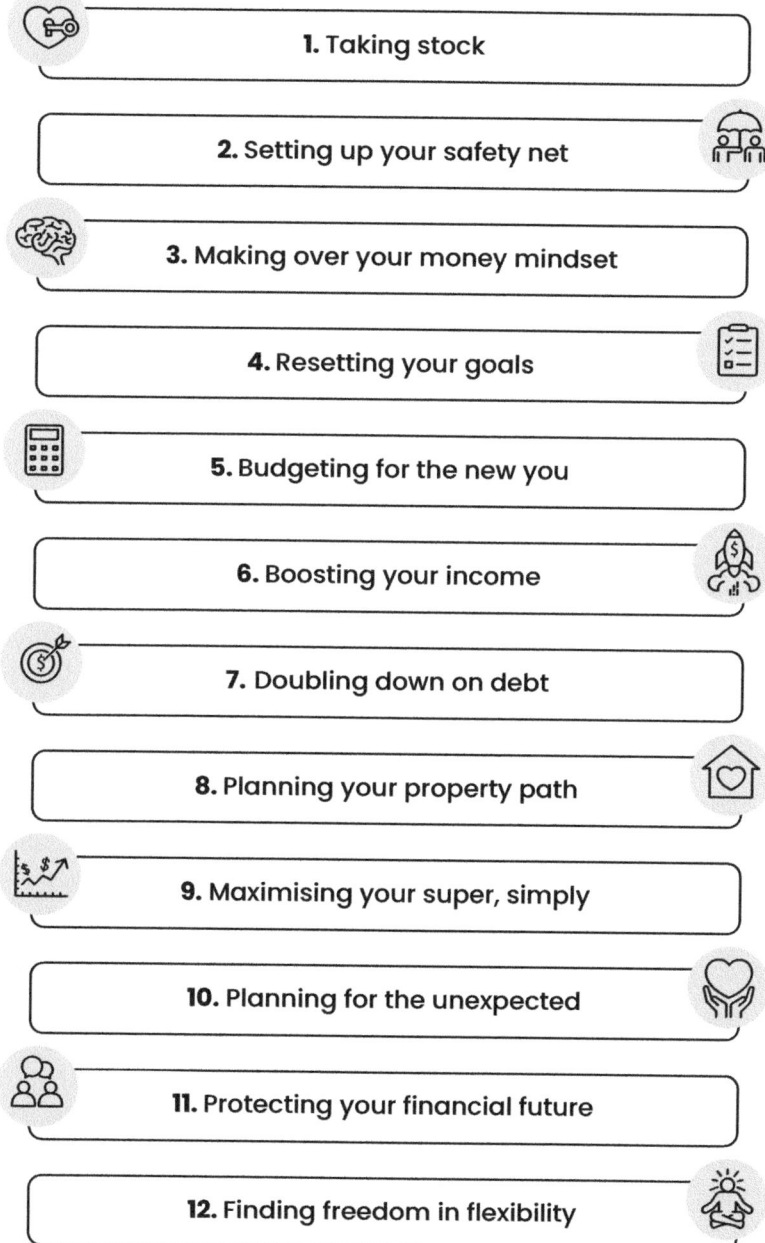

1. Taking stock

2. Setting up your safety net

3. Making over your money mindset

4. Resetting your goals

5. Budgeting for the new you

6. Boosting your income

7. Doubling down on debt

8. Planning your property path

9. Maximising your super, simply

10. Planning for the unexpected

11. Protecting your financial future

12. Finding freedom in flexibility

CONCLUSION

Well done. You've made it!

Whether it took you 12 weeks, 12 months or longer to read, think about or action the ideas in this book, remember: Money isn't a one-and-done thing.

Everything in this book is something you'll keep coming back to, tweaking and adjusting as life shifts. Some parts might have been easy, others might have felt like a slog. But every step you took was a step towards more clarity, confidence and control over your financial future.

Along the way, you've been building a foundation that isn't just solid — it's *flexible*. Real financial security isn't about sticking to rigid rules or perfect plans. It's about creating options. It's about financial flexibility.

Life may keep throwing curveballs, but the difference now is that you won't be starting from scratch next time. You'll be starting from a place of strength, resilience and experience. Whether it's a career shift, an unexpected expense or a major life transition, you now have the tools to adjust, reset and keep moving forward.

And you don't have to do it alone. Your village — the people who support, guide and encourage you — will continue to be your greatest asset. Whether it's friends, family, professionals or your own inner circle of trusted advisers, lean on them when you need to.

When things feel tough, remember the slingshot. Sometimes, life pulls you back with unexpected expenses, a career shift or a challenge you didn't see coming. But now, that pullback isn't a setback. It's just momentum building before you launch forward, stronger than before.

Connect with me

Love what you've learned here? Let's take it further.

You've done the work to reset, rebuild and regain control of your financial future, and now it's time to take things to the next level. Whether you're looking for deeper financial education, practical tools or a supportive community, there is something for every age and stage.

- *Learn with me:* Ready to go beyond the book? Access my coaching, courses and free resources to help you refine your strategy, take action and build a future that you love.

- *Listen in:* Keep the momentum going with the *Australian Finance Podcast,* where I dive deeper into money mindset, smart financial moves and wealth-building strategies every week

- *Join the community:* Surround yourself with like-minded people who are also resetting their financial future. Find insights, tools and conversations at gemmamitchell.com.au.

Your comeback story is just beginning. Let's build your next chapter together.

Follow along:

LinkedIn: linkedin.com/in/gemma-mitchell

Instagram: instagram.com/gemmamitchell.finance

Facebook: facebook.com/gemmamitchell.finance

YouTube: youtube.com/@gemmamitchellCFC

ACKNOWLEDGEMENTS

They say it takes a village, and I couldn't agree more. This book wouldn't exist without the incredible people I'm lucky enough to call my village — the ones who've had my back, lifted me up and reminded me why I do what I do.

To my family and friends: Thank you for being my safe place, my sounding board and my reality check. You never stop showing up — for me, my kids and my work — and your support means everything. Over the last two very difficult years, you made sure I got up, ate, exercised (even when it was the last thing I wanted to do) and, most importantly, encouraged me to start writing. This book exists because of you.

My ex-husband, Alex: I'm grateful that our kids have such a wonderful dad. I'm thankful for the way we co-parent and proud of the life we built together for them and for ourselves. Your ongoing support allows me to travel and do the work that lights me up, and that doesn't go unnoticed. Thank you.

To my professional network, mentors and peers — so many of whom I've met through the wonderful and wild world of social media: Thank you for reigniting my passion for finance when I was completely burned out and ready to walk away. I'm beyond grateful to be surrounded by such brilliant, inspirational minds.

And to every client I've been lucky enough to work with, and to you, the reader holding this book: You are the reason I wrote it. I hope it gives you clarity, confidence and the belief that no financial setback is ever the end of your story.

Finally, thank you to Lucy Raymond and Kelly Irvine: Without you, this book wouldn't be what it is today. Thank you for believing in me and *The Money Reset*.

With gratitude,
Gemma

ADDITIONAL
RESOURCES

No matter where you are in your journey, it's important to remember that support is available to help you navigate the financial, legal and emotional complexities of life transitions.

Whether you're restructuring your finances after a life event or simply seeking to enhance your financial stability, tapping into the right support services can help you move forward with confidence and clarity.

Here are some other essential support services that can provide guidance and assistance:

Family and financial support

- *Family Relationship Advice Line:* Helps with family issues and separation, referring you to local services for further assistance. Call 1800 050 321 or visit familyrelationships.gov.au.

- *1800RESPECT:* This national family violence and sexual assault counselling service operates 24/7, offering confidential, free support. It also provides advice on online safety if you suspect someone is monitoring your online activity. Visit 1800respect.org.au for more information.

- *Moneysmart:* Offers guidance on managing your finances, urgent money help and information on divorce and separation. Visit moneysmart.gov.au.

- *National Debt Helpline:* For debt problems, you can call 1800 007 007 or visit ndh.org.au.

- *National Legal Aid:* Connects you to the Legal Aid commission in your state or territory. For more information, visit nationallegalaid.org.au.

Support for people with disabilities

- *Disability Gateway:* Provides information on family and domestic violence, and connects you to support services for people with disabilities. Visit disabilitygateway.gov.au for more details.

- *National Disability Abuse and Neglect Hotline:* To report neglect and abuse of people with disabilities, call 1800 880 052.

- *Women With Disabilities Australia (WWDA):* Advocates for women, girls and non-binary individuals with disabilities, working to promote human rights and end all forms of discrimination. Learn more at wwda.org.au.

LGBTIQ+ and family resources

- *LGBTIQ+ Health Australia:* For multiple resources supporting lesbian, gay, bisexual, trans/transgender, intersex, queer and other sexuality, gender and bodily diverse people and communities throughout Australia and the world, free from stigma and discrimination, visit lgbtiqhealth.org.au.

Resources for children

- *Raising Children Network:* Provides a list of helplines and resources for children experiencing abuse. Visit raisingchildren.net.au for further support.

Elder abuse support

- *1800 ELDERHelp Line:* The Elder Abuse Help Line (1800 353 374) connects you to your state or territory service for assistance with elder abuse. Hours of operation vary.

- *Compass:* A national website with resources about the abuse of older Australians. You can find support services near you by visiting compass.info.

GLOSSARY OF FINANCIAL SPECIALISTS

Here's a breakdown of experts you might lean on during different stages of your wealth journey — whether you're laying foundations, growing your assets or protecting what you've built.

Building your financial village doesn't mean you're handing over control, it means surrounding yourself with the right supports so you can make informed, confident decisions. Having the right people in your corner makes all the difference when it comes to navigating financial transitions and building lasting wealth.

Accountant

Accountants are essential for tax planning, financial reporting and structuring your tax affairs effectively. They ensure you maximise tax benefits and plan for long-term success.

Buyer's agent

Unlike a real estate agent who works for people selling properties, buyers agents work solely for property buyers, assisting with finding, evaluating and negotiating purchases. They're particularly helpful in competitive markets.

Centrelink financial information service (FIS) officer

Centrelink FIS officers provide free advice about how your financial decisions could impact current or future Centrelink payments. They're a great resource for understanding entitlements and strategies. Find out more at servicesaustralia.gov.au/centrelink.

Estate planning lawyer

An estate planning lawyer helps protect your assets and ensures your wishes are followed after you die. They assist with wills, powers of attorney and trusts to secure your legacy.

Family lawyer

Family lawyers provide guidance on matters like separation, divorce, custody and financial settlements. They ensure your rights are protected as you navigate shared finances or property divisions.

Financial adviser

A financial adviser (or planner) is there to help you make smart, informed decisions about your money—from investing and super to planning for retirement and everything in between. They'll help you get clear on your goals and understand your options. And they'll provide strategic advice on how to get there — including what products (like investments or insurance) you might need to support the plan.

Caution: In Australia, financial advisers must be licensed and registered, meeting strict regulatory standards. Check the financial adviser register at moneysmart.gov.au.

Financial and debt counsellor

If you're struggling to make ends meet, a financial counsellor offers support with debt management, creditor negotiations, Centrelink entitlements and even bankruptcy. Their services are typically free for those who meet eligibility criteria through resources like the National Debt Helpline (ndh.org.au).

Mortgage broker

A mortgage broker helps you secure the best loan for your needs, whether you're buying, refinancing or investing, and will consider all of your options across multiple banks and lenders. Note that a bank lender works for their institution, while a broker works for you.

Real estate agent

A real estate agent helps you sell or lease property, managing marketing, negotiations and transactions using their local market expertise.

Tax agent

Tax agents focus specifically on preparing and lodging tax returns, ensuring compliance with Australian Taxation Office (ATO) requirements. Unlike an accountant, they aren't generally qualified to give you strategic tax advice.

Wealth coach

A wealth coach focuses on financial education, helping you build good habits, set goals and stay accountable. They work on foundational money management strategies such as budgeting, cashflow and mindset.

Caution: Wealth coaches in Australia aren't required to have formal qualifications, so vet their experience carefully.

How to find the right professional for you

Finding professionals who not only have the expertise but also align with your values, goals and communication style can be tricky, and chances are you'll need to speak to a few.

Don't be afraid to interview potential professionals. Talk to a few and compare their approaches. Here are some questions you might consider:

- What are your qualifications and how is your industry regulated?
- What's your experience working with clients in situations like mine?
- How do you typically work with your clients?

- What's your philosophy or approach to (specific topic, e.g., investing, budgeting or debt management)?

- What kind of support can I expect, and how often will we communicate?

- How are your fees structured, and what value do you deliver for those fees?

You're not just hiring a service; you're building a relationship. Choose someone who listens, understands your unique situation and explains things in a way that makes sense to you.

Trust your instincts — if something doesn't feel right, keep looking. The right professional will make you feel confident, supported and empowered to reach your financial goals.

Wanting to keep DIY-ing your learning?

Learning about finances can be empowering, and how you learn is just as important as what you learn. Some people love podcasts, YouTube videos or self-paced courses, while others prefer live sessions or getting lost in a good finance book. The real challenge isn't a lack of information — there's an overwhelming amount out there — it's figuring out *who to trust* and how to sort the good from the garbage.

When choosing where to learn, check the:

- *Experience:* Look for experts with a proven track record and a reputation for integrity.

- *Credentials:* Do they have the expertise and qualifications?

The right resources and mentors make a huge difference, so be open to knowing when you can DIY and when it's worth getting expert help.

My personal recommendation: If you're looking for trusted, high-quality financial education, I highly recommend the *Australian Finance Podcast* and Rask Education (yes, I may be biased, but honestly, I referred friends, family and clients to them long before I started working with them). They offer excellent free content and courses to support you at every stage of your financial journey. Go check them out — you won't regret it!

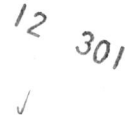

Printed and bound by CPI Group (UK) Ltd, Croydon, CR0 4YY

06/08/2025

14714619-0001